THE SWEETNESS

THE SWEETNESS

Stories by
Ninamaste MaTuri

ISBN 978-1-300-94136-1

Other books in
The Gerbera Series

The Preludes
Clear Sense

I give big thanks to my family and friends for their love and support from the start to finish of this book.

Contents

ANCHORED

MELANIE

CHAPTER ONE

A rust-colored leaf fell from a tree and spiraled down towards the hood of a white car. Once it landed, it vibrated from the bass of The Killers's "Somebody Told Me" as the song blared from the vehicle's stereo. The vibration and music stopped when the sedan's engine turned off. The leaf vibrated once again upon slams of three of the car's doors. The sounds of a pair of heels tapping on the parking lot asphalt mingled with the sounds of birds chirping. A single-engine plane flying above Kansas City, Missouri could also be heard. One of the high heeltaps was muffled by a gum wrapper discarded by the person walking in front who had on a pair of brown sandals. A pair of sneakers held a glass door open as the pair of heels and sandals walked through. The trio made their way down a floral patterned carpeted corridor. They walked through a door that held a sign that read: Rental Office.

"I received the cashier's check for a full year's rent," a woman with curly, red hair said as she looked over the lease agreement she held in her hands. The woman's green eyes scanned the signatures then read the first names: Melanie, Karen, and Keith. "I must say it isn't everyday we receive a full year's rent. It's especially out of the ordinary the signee isn't related to any of you," the woman said suspiciously.

No one responded to the woman's comment. The woman set the lease down on her desk then folded her hands atop the document. Her green eyes focused on Melanie to her left. She took in her medium-sized Afro that looked like a light brown, fluffy halo. The woman made eye contact but soon looked away when her eyes met the penetrating glare of the Afro's keeper. The woman's eyes then rested upon Karen whose blonde hair fell straight down to her delicate shoulders. She then looked farther to her right at a lock of curly blonde hair that was being twirled by Keith. His body had a gentle rocking motion as his upper leg, which was crossed on top of the other, swayed back and forth. The scent of his grape-flavored gum filled the air between them.

The woman sighed then said, "We have a zero tolerance for things like drugs, prostitution, and wild parties on this property."

The young man stopped twirling his lock of hair and coolly folded his hands. He then said with a confident nod, "That sounds like the kind of place we'll feel comfortable to call home."

The woman gave one last look at the three of them. She noted that the only thing they all had in common was that they were in their early twenties. The woman sighed. The disbelief of what she was about to do caused her to push air from her nostrils in a quick spurt. She handed each of them a key and said, "Well, welcome to your new home."

CHAPTER TWO

"Melanie, do you have the coke? And where the hell is Karen? Dat bitch betta have my money!"

"Okay, Pimp Keith, you party animal you." The corniness of her words caused Melanie to burst out in laughter.

"Oh my goodness, did she really think we're some motley crew of society's rejects?" Karen said as she began to unpack a box that had the word kitchen written on it.

Keith cut opened the bottom of another box. He then flattened it. "Apparently, she's never seen cousins before," he muttered.

"Keith, you're awesome though. I was about to go off on her when you said—" Karen joined Melanie in the recital, "That sounds like the kind of place we'll feel comfortable to call home."

"Yeah, well, when you're gender and sex are at opposite ends, you learn how to handle bullshit when it's thrown at you. Mel, you should know that lesson as well."

"I'm still learning. Say, where's that box marked memories?"

Karen walked over to the balcony door where the box lay. "We can't open it until we have everything unpacked and put away," Karen said as she pushed the box to the corner of their new living room. Karen walked back to the balcony door and placed her hands on her slim hips. "This is so cool. I never thought we would have such an amazing view."

Melanie walked to Karen's side. She too began to enjoy the view of a pond that had geese swimming in it. The brightness of the sun glistening on the water was almost blinding.

Keith squeezed his slender body between his cousins then wrapped his arms around both of their shoulders. He then said, "Thank you, Keith, for this amazing apartment. If it wasn't for you, I would be living with my annoying girlfriend." Keith looked at Melanie. He then continued, "And, I would be living with my parents who drink and bitch all day about people they love to hate." Keith then looked at Karen.

Melanie shook her head. "Yes, thank you for saving me from a life with the annoying girlfriend," she kissed Keith on his cheek. "Though, I do miss my boo," Melanie continued.

"When does she get back from Miami?" Keith asked.

"She gets back this weekend. I can't wait to show her our new pad," Melanie said excitedly.

"Ah, Mel misses her boo," Karen said sarcastically. "Anyways, let's back it up. Why are you thanking, Keith? It's the good doctor, Keith's one and only, we should thank," Karen said.

"But, if it wasn't for my…"

"Butt," Melanie said as she gently squeezed Keith's right butt cheek.

Keith clinched his cheeks and gave a slight chuckle. He then said, "To sum it up, yeah."

The following evening was filled with the sounds of the last bits of unpacking. Melanie, Karen, and Keith were placing their final treasured items in their respective bedrooms. Melanie sat on her bed as she wiped the picture frame that contained a photo of her and her girlfriend. They were on a beach in a loving embrace during sunset. She kissed the picture then placed it on her nightstand. Karen placed her remaining high heels on a shoe hanger that hung from the back of her closet door. Keith stuffed the packaging from his new bedding into a big black trash bag.

Keith then hulled the bag from his master bedroom down the hall. He stopped at Karen's bedroom door. "Do you think we can open the memory box now?"

"Yes," Karen said. She grabbed a box cutter from her dresser.

Keith continued down the hall to Melanie's room. He didn't stop walking when he yelled, "Time capsule time!"

Karen and Melanie walked swiftly to the box that was still in the corner of the living room. They pushed it to the middle of the room between the entertainment center and coffee table. They all kneeled down around it. Karen clapped her hands together and said, "Okay, so now I've kept some mementos throughout our years and placed it in this box not too long ago. Are you guys ready to see what's in the box?"

Melanie waved her hands in the air as if she were swatting flies away from her face. "Girl, would you stop with the suspense and get to it," she said eager to see what was hiding behind the brown cardboard.

Karen took a box cutter and slid it across the tape that was on top of the time capsule. She reached in and took out a picture of the three of them at Melanie's tenth birthday party.

"Oh, I remember this," Keith said. "This was when I had to teach you a lesson about meddling in other people's business."

"Yes, a lesson I still remember to this day. What goes around comes around."

Karen reached into the box again. She pulled out a letter that was folded into an origami style square.

"Oh no, don't tell me you kept that," Melanie said. Her cheeks became red.

Karen nodded with eyebrows raised. "Uh huh, let's see here," Karen said as she began to unfold the letter.

Melanie snatched it from her.

"Please don't. That was so embarrassing. It's one of those moments I wish I could erase." Melanie clinched the paper in her right hand.

"Okay, we won't read it," Karen said.

"Is that the letter we were going to give to Tiffany after you ruined the relationship with her man? What was his name?"

"Michael," Karen helped out.

"Yes, Michael. Tiffany, Melanie's first crush, or rather your first victim. Ruined the girl's relationship just so you could have her. Then when it was over you didn't want her anymore. That was after you found out she was pregnant by her man. Oh what webs we spin for ourselves." Keith shook his head in an exaggerated way.

"Then we write a letter to right the wrong but never sent it to her," Karen continued the story as she looked at the note in Melanie's hand.

"It was better to leave well enough alone," Melanie said plaintively.

"Yeah, well, they ended up back together without us meddling around any further," Keith said.

"Thankfully," Melanie said then handed the letter back to Karen. Karen set it aside. "Speaking of that time period. Keith, did you ever see that Rome guy again?"

"I never saw him but I did see his secret lover again a few times. He told me Rome and his girlfriend ended up moving down here from Detroit," Keith said.

"He had a girlfriend?" Karen asked.

"Did she know about his bisexual ways?" Melanie asked, interrupting Keith's response to Karen.

"Yes, he had a girlfriend. And no, Rome used to rendezvous with secret lover man, Jake, whenever he could."

"Oh no, did he end up getting HIV from Jake?" Melanie asked.

Karen said, "The bug-chaser," as a way to correct the description of Jake.

"I have no idea if Rome got it. I wanted to ask Jake, but it was one of those things I just didn't want to know. Especially since Rome had a girlfriend. Karen, yes, he was a bug-chaser."

"Can't people go to jail for infecting someone with HIV?" Karen asked.

"In some places, yes. That is if the infected person knew and the non-infected person didn't know," Keith answered.

"That poor girl," Melanie said in a solemn tone.

The cousins sat quiet for a moment.

Melanie broke the moment of silence. "Karen do you have any happy memories in this time capsule of yours?"

Karen chuckled lightly. "I know, right? As a matter of fact I do."

Melanie and Keith repositioned themselves in anticipation of the next memento that would be lifted from the time capsule.

The trio spent the rest of evening enjoying the retelling of past stories and touching items they hadn't seen in years. They also enjoyed spending time with the people they loved the most, each other.

CHAPTER THREE

Melanie's right hand slid across the mahogany banister as she followed Nneka down the stairs of an historic three-story apartment building. Melanie held her sketchpad and drawing utensils in her left hand. Nneka also carried a sketchpad and utensils. The warm and woody scent of Egyptian Musk lifted from the sides of Nneka's neck, glided through her shoulder-length black kinky, twist-styled hair, and swept across Melanie's nose. The clip-clop sounds Nneka's black flip-flops made echoed in the stairwell.

"I can't wait to see the dungeon that provides you with so much inspiration," Melanie said.

Nneka kept her eyes on the steps in front of her as she said, "Whatever, Mel. We're almost there."

"I mean come on Neek ... the basement. There can be zero inspiration found from being underground with zilch natural light. Not to mention the claustrophobia that would begin to set in."

"Speak for yourself. My little space suits me just fine. Plus, it gives me the opportunity to get away from my roommate who goes on and on about how great her love life is."

Nneka continued holding a bit of her ankle-length, lavender-colored wrap skirt to help ensure it didn't cause her a tumble down the remaining set of stairs.

"And here we are."

The ladies stood in a hall in the finished basement. There were three doors. The sounds from the washer and dryer could be heard but not seen from one end of the hall. At the other end of the hall was a wall that contained a large painting of chardonnay grapes hanging on a vine in a vineyard. Nneka walked to the middle door with Melanie close behind. Melanie was surprised the space lacked the usual basement damp scent and feel.

Nneka took a key that dangled from an elastic bracelet that contained cedar wood beads from her wrist. She unlocked the door and invited Melanie in. A white walled room covered in Nneka's sketches greeted Melanie. Cherry wood colored laminate floors anchored the room. A bright light in the center of the ceiling was courtesy of the landlord, a fellow artist, who installed the recessed lighting. Light also came in from a small window near the ceiling, courtesy of the sunshine. There was an assortment of shade-loving green plants in three of the corners. Between them, lay a collection of large throw pillows, and a contemporary maroon loveseat sat against one wall. It faced an electric cherry wood fireplace that stood about halfway up Melanie's five-foot-seven frame.

Hung above the fireplace was a drawing that Nneka had done. It was of her mother, a year before she had given birth to Nneka. Nneka used a photo she had found while going through a family album. The picture captivated her because her mother's smile reminded her of her own delicate smile. There was also a love that radiated from her eyes. The feeling was not directed towards the camera but rather towards whoever had taken the photo. Curious, Nneka went into the kitchen where her mother and father were reading their favorite sections of the local newspaper. Her mother's favorite section was arts and entertainment. Politics was her father's favorite section. They were enjoying each other's company, though they were silent. Nneka placed the picture on the table and asked who took it. Her father continued reading while her mother lowered the paper. She glanced at the photo and said in an enduring tone, "Your father." Nneka's father lowered his section of the paper, upon hearing the response and the tone in his wife's voice. He looked at the picture smiled warmly and then continued reading the paper.

Nneka watched Melanie look over items in her studio. She also took in Melanie's choppy uneven Afro. "So what do you think?" Nneka asked.

"I must say I am impressed. Your landlord sure did hook you up. Are all three like this?"

"No, they are all different depending on whoever is renting the space."

"Well, I like your style."

Nneka smiled. "Speaking of style, what plans do you have for your hair?" Nneka asked.

Melanie went farther into the room looking over the plants and pillows. She then sat down on the loveseat while Nneka locked the door.

"What do you mean by plans?" Melanie responded.

Nneka walked over to the pile of pillows and sat. Melanie watched her as she opened her sketchpad to a blank page and chose her pencils. "I mean there is no real style to it. I never really have seen you do something with it."

"I don't know what I should do with it? I hate my hair. It's just there. A big round bush on top of my head," Melanie said.

"Will you let me put some cornrows in it for you?" Nneka asked.

"Sure. I've never had that done before," Melanie said.

"You never had it done?"

"Nope. Never knew anyone who could do it."

"The joys of being bi-racial and being brought up with your white side of the family, huh?"

"Yeah, something like that," Melanie said. She looked distant when she responded.

Nneka was about give Melanie a hard time about the white side of her family but decided not to when she saw Melanie's expression. Instead she said, "Well, today is your lucky day." She then winked. Nneka saw Melanie's expression brighten up. Nneka continued speaking, "But before we do that let me do this."

Nneka propped her sketchpad on her lap.

"Ready?" Nneka said.

"What? That's your process? Lock door, walk over to pillows, sit, ask questions about my hair, then ready?"

"What is it supposed to be?"

"I don't know maybe some candles, a little jazz music, some incense. You know get in the mood kind of stuff."

Nneka wrinkled her forehead and said, "That sounds like the baby-making process to me," she smirked and shook her head.

Melanie narrowed her eyes towards Nneka in a sexy way.

"Would you consider your art your baby?"

"Yeah, I guess so."

"So would you say that you and I are about to enter into the baby-making process."

Nneka's dark brown skin hid the fact that her cheeks turned beet red. The ever so observant Melanie noticed the usually confident demeanor of Nneka melt into bashfulness. *Beautiful*, Melanie thought.

"You're crazy," Nneka said in a barely audible voice as she fidgeted with a pencil.

Melanie began to hum the tune to Billie Holiday's "Crazy He Calls Me."

"Sure, I'm crazy. Crazy in love I say," Melanie sung aloud to the tune in her head. With a slow and deliberate movement, she stood up, walked over to the fireplace, and turned on the light and not the heat. Melanie then turned the studio light off and sat back down. Her singing turned into a hum as she opened her sketchpad to a blank sheet and selected a pencil. Melanie closed her eyes and inhaled deeply the scent of Egyptian Musk that seemed to be coming stronger from Nneka. She opened her eyes and looked at Nneka with an intensity that Nneka hadn't seen before. It was as if Melanie could see every cell inside her body and that she loved what she saw.

"I thought I was going to draw you and I was going to look at some of your work. Maybe get some tips?" Nneka said in a weak voice.

Melanie didn't respond right away. Instead she concentrated on the difficulty of trying to communicate Nneka's rare aura at that moment onto her pad.

"Later," Melanie responded.

"When?"

Melanie rose from the loveseat. She went over to Nneka and gave her a soft kiss on her lips. Nneka's bashfulness intensified. *There it is,* Melanie thought.

With the continued slow and deliberate movement, Melanie went back to her seat with sketchpad and pencil in hand.

"The difficult I'll do right now. The impossible will take a little while." Melanie continued singing in a soft tone.

A little later, after Melanie completed her drawing, Nneka was sitting on her studio's loveseat with Melanie sitting between her legs on the floor. Her dress was hiked up to her knees, revealing manicured toenails with clear nail polish and a set of soft brown legs. Nneka rubbed the strong woody scent of Carol's Daughter Khoret Amen hair oil into her hands then began massaging it into Melanie's hair. She then picked up a wide toothcomb, sectioned Melanie's coarse hair, and began detangling. Nneka was surprised that Melanie did not say anything as she began working the knots out.

"I can't believe you're not tender-headed," Nneka said.

"What does that mean?"

"You don't know what tender-headed means?" Nneka said in disbelief.

"No, I don't."

"It means you're not saying ouch when I comb the naps out."

"What are naps?"

"Melanie, you have got to be joking."

Melanie did not say anything. She just sat quiet while the feeling of embarrassment rolled through her body.

"Naps are the knots or tangles that I am picking out. Black folks and other kinds of folks call them naps. Didn't you ever hang with your dad's side of the family?"

"Nope. They had nothing to do with him when he married my mom. He hasn't spoken to them since before I was born." Melanie sighed.

Nneka finished combing through Melanie's hair. She began parting her hair into wavy sections. "Did you ever wonder about them?"

"Of course I did. You know, it wasn't always the greatest growing up the only person of color in a family. I stood out in family pictures with my cousins. Always had to explain why I was so dark and my cousins were white. But now ... I don't know."

There was a moment of silence. Nneka tried to gauge what Melanie was feeling and thinking but could not. She finished the third row and began working on the fourth.

"What kind of woman have you dated?" Nneka asked breaking the silence.

Melanie gave a cool smile and began nodding her head back and forth. "Dark-skinned black. As they say, the blacker the berry the sweeter the juice." Melanie took her right hand and threaded it between the loveseat and Nneka's leg. Melanie began stroking Nneka's soft leg in approval.

Nneka giggled softly. "My question related more to personality."

"I can't help it. My mind is going to those certain places."

"Well, not now. Later."

"When?"

Nneka gave a sly smile. "When I am done with your hair." She began working on the seventh row and estimated that she had about five more to go. "The difficult I'll do right now. The impossible will take a little while." Nneka sang in a soft tone.

Melanie smiled, giving Nneka's calf a soft squeeze.

Chapter Four

The following morning, Melanie walked into GEB. It was a food distribution company where she worked as a warehouse supervisor. She inhaled the air as she walked into the building. She enjoyed the scent of cardboard mixed in the air with the scent of diesel fuel. She also enjoyed the sights of the semi-trucks rolling in with deliverables and rolling out with orders. The smells and sights made her feel masculine.

Melanie went to her desk and looked at her calendar for the day. There was one thing written for that day, training. She rolled her eyes. Melanie wondered how she could have forgotten about the training she was going to have to do that day. She felt uneasy about doing it because of her strong feelings about how the new person got the job as a selector in the first place, which was by way of her manager being a friend of someone in the new-hire's family. No interview with Melanie, not even an opinion asked. Just her manager informing her that a person named Mike would be starting on such and such a day. "Let's get this done," Melanie said to herself.

Melanie knew where to find the new guy. It was a place that the newbies were usually sent as they walked around the large warehouse wondering where to go. Melanie entered the break room. Sure enough sitting with his hands clasped together and left leg bouncing uncontrollably was an unfamiliar man. He had on baggy jeans, a hooded blue sweatshirt that had a grey T-shirt peeking through the top of the front zipper. Though he was covered from head to toe Melanie could see he was in shape by his posture and chiseled facial features. She walked to the vending machine and punched in her selection for Mountain Dew after inserting her bills. She then took a step to her left and selected a Snickers from the snack machine. Melanie took a deep breath in an attempt to get herself pumped up to do what she had no desire to do. Train someone, whom in her mind, probably thought he was privileged and would not work hard because he has friends in high places. She cracked open her can of soda. The sound made the man stop bouncing his leg and look up. The two made eye contact with one another.

"You have got to be shittin' me!" the man exclaimed.

Melanie looked startled.

"You don't recognize me, do you?"

"Am I supposed to?"

"Maybe if I do this it will ring a bell."

The man stood up from his chair placed his hands under his shirt to make it look like he was pregnant. He then puffed air into his cheeks like he was Louis Armstrong creating high notes through a trumpet. Melanie stood dumbfounded. Thoughts of how this guy was not only privileged and lazy but also insane floated through Melanie's mind.

The man stopped his gestures as he saw his clues weren't hitting home for Melanie. He said, "Mel, you really don't remember me? Hell, I know I've changed but I didn't think by that much. How's your cousin, Karen? Is she still evil?"

New thoughts floated through Melanie's mind. She figured she must know him if he knew her name. It must have been from a long time ago for him to refer to Karen as mean since she's totally changed. Still, nothing came to her.

"Dude, who the hell are you? Enough dumb clues and hints. How do I know you and my cousin?"

"Because, we went to school together. We even had Christmas together when my old man had a heart attack." The man again blew air into his cheeks and placed is hands under his sweatshirt like he was pregnant.

Home run.

"Big Mike?" Melanie shouted. She placed her soda and candy on a table and rushed to him. The two former friends gave each other a big hug.

"Man you *have* changed. You look great. Wait until I tell Karen! What's new? What have you been up to?"

"Okay, let's see here. How do I sum up years into a few sentences? After school was out that year my family moved to Overland Park, Kansas. I got tired of being called fat and not being able to keep up in gym. I proceeded to lose weight and build up these guns." Mike flexed his biceps under his sweatshirt then continued to say, "The hotties have been all over me ever since."

"Cool man. So your pops is okay?"

"He is as healthy as a horse, as they say."

"Good to hear. So what brings you back to Kansas City?"

Mike rubbed his nose, "Well, I decided to try to settle down with one of those hotties. She wasn't feeling it. Said she wanted to explore all of her available options. Whatever that means. Broken heart, shattered dreams, and memories. I had to get out of there and start new someplace else."

"Hey, I hear you. There's no place like home."

Mike smiled, "Exactly. So, what about you? What have you been up to?"

"Not much just working these days. Suppose to be training you in today as a matter of fact."

"Get out! For real?"

"Yup."

"So, what's up with Karen?"

"The same way I didn't recognize you, you would not recognize Karen, personality-wise."

"Why, is she even more evil than before? Is she like the devil or some shit?"

Melanie laughed. "No. Just the opposite."

"What she an angel? Is she dead?"

Melanie laughed harder. She managed to say, "No she is alive and well. She just doesn't act that way anymore. She stepped on one too many toes and was pretty much forced to change."

"Yeah, I remember when she smashed that cake in my face at your birthday party. You remember that? That was messed up, man." Mike started to laugh.

Tears began to form in Melanie's eyes. "That was funny as hell."

"It wasn't funny then, but now I can laugh."

The two friends' laughter slowed.

"Just like old times," Melanie said.

"Yup, just like old times. So how is your love life? Any broken hearts, shattered dreams and memories like mine?" Mike said.

"My love life is complicated," Melanie said.

"Sooo you with a female or what?"

Melanie looked surprised.

"Come on, Mel. It's all good. You weren't the most feminine girl back in school and looking at you now." Mike looked over Melanie's men jeans and Timberland boots.

"Yeah, I got me a girl," Melanie replied.

Another worker overheard Melanie's comment as he walked into the break room.

"Melanie's girl is hella fine!" he exclaimed. "A dark-skinned lovely with juicy kissable lips, and a fat—"

"Yo, yo, yo, man," Melanie interrupted.

The man threw his arms up in surrender. He lowered his right hand down and placed it across his chest. "No harm. Just saying your lady is fine." The man grabbed bottled water from the refrigerator and left.

"Wow, that doesn't sound complicated at all. What's her name?"

Melanie felt the warmth of pride spread over her. She knew her girlfriend was gorgeous, and Melanie loved the fact that others saw that as well.

"It's not I guess. Just gotta deal with knuckleheads like that a lot. Her name is Chantal." Melanie's mind drifted momentarily to her enjoyment of spending time with Nneka the day before. She quickly snapped out of it and said, "Hey, you have to come over soon and see Karen. We're roommates. She is going to hit the floor when she sees you. In the meantime, how about you and I do a happy hour and get caught up?"

"Of course to both. I would really like to see this new and improved cousin of yours."

"Well, what are you doing Saturday night? Karen, Keith and his boyfriend, my girl, and I are going out to bowl."

"I'm down. It is no surprise that Keith has a boyfriend. He stroked Princess Leia's hair one too many times when he got those *Star Wars* collectibles."

Melanie smiled. "Yeah. Anyways, let's get you trained. I wasn't sure how this day was going to go but I see it's going to be a good one."

CHAPTER FIVE

The sun's rays beamed at nine o'clock in the morning on Saturday. Melanie stretched. She felt the warmth of Chantal next to her. She turned to face her. Melanie took in her perfectly arched eyebrows and long eyelashes. She placed her thumb on the sides of Chantal's hairline. Melanie began to slide her thumb softly down the side to her jawbone. Chantal's eyes flickered open. She peered into Melanie's eyes. Chantal placed her hand over her mouth to try and mask her morning breath as she said, "Good morning, baby. What time did you get in last night?"

"About midnight," Melanie replied.

"An extended happy hour, huh? Well did you have fun?"

"Of course. The boys and I always have fun when we get together."

"That's good," Chantal removed the peach and sage-colored comforter from her body then said, "I gotta use the restroom."

Melanie watched as Chantal exited the bed and headed to the guest bathroom. She enjoyed seeing the backside of her voluptuous girlfriend. Her butt bounced and switched under her coral-colored boy shorts as she walked away. Melanie soaked in the way the color of her shorts complimented her skin complexion.

Melanie got out of bed and headed to the living room. She saw Karen doing the downward-facing dog yoga pose on her purple yoga mat. Karen walked both of her manicured feet to her hands and moved into a forward bend pose. Her pointy tail dangled from the back of her head. Melanie proceeded to the kitchen where she went to the refrigerator, retrieved orange juice that had her name written on it, and drank from the carton. She walked to the pass-through of the kitchen and looked at Karen who was now in a cross-legged seated pose in prayer position with her eyes closed.

"All done," Melanie said.

Karen opened her eyes.

"Hey you, you were missed last night. Keith and the good doctor kicked our butts. I barely broke a hundred. I just kept rolling one gutter ball after another. Your girl kept us above water though with a 129. Needless to say, I'll be working hard to get my average up tonight."

Melanie thought about revealing Mike coming along but decided to keep it a surprise.

"That's my girl," Melanie said.

"That's your girl, what?" a fully dressed Chantal asked as she walked into the living room.

Melanie's eyes looked over her girlfriend as if they were a pair of scanners at a checkout lane. Melanie checked out Chantal's straight brown hair with golden bronze highlights that was shaped into a bob: $125. Manicured eyebrows, fingernails, and toes: $85. She had on a green peasant dress by a designer that Melanie could not pronounce: $250. Melanie clinched her teeth with the thought of how much she had spent for the look that stood before her. She then looked at the beautiful face that set lust ablaze in her body. The flawless makeup that accented Chantal's high cheekbones and punctuated her lips was something she didn't pay for. Chantal worked as a freelance makeup artist and had a cache of everything to make a person look like they had a black eye to making them look and feel like royalty in their own made-up kingdom.

"Karen was just telling me how you were able to save the game last night," Melanie said as she attempted to give Chantal a peck on her cheek.

Chantal snapped her head back away from Melanie. "Mel, you're kidding me right? You really think I wanna kiss you with your morning breath and OJ cocktail? Why don't you go wash up before you drink?"

"Because, I don't like the taste of mint toothpaste with my juice."

"Don't waste your time, Chantal. Melanie's been doing that since the beginning of time," Karen said as she rolled up her yoga mat.

"I guess I am beginning to learn a few new things about you now that I'm staying the night."

"Me too."

"Like what?"

"Like how fine you look in the morning."

"Oh, thank you, baby. I would give you a kiss but, you know," Chantal said as she smirked.

Karen walked up to Melanie. She pinched one of her cheeks through the pass-through as she said, "Oh, Melanie," in a sarcastic tone as she walked to her bedroom. *You're so full of shit,* Karen thought.

Chantal narrowed her eyes a bit in Karen's direction as she was puzzled by her tone. She turned her attention to Melanie who seemed to be oblivious to Chantal's puzzlement. Chantal told herself it was nothing since Melanie did not seem to react to Karen's sarcasm. "Why don't you go wash up," Chantal said.

"Fine," Melanie placed the juice back in the refrigerator then retreated to the bathroom to wash up.

Melanie lathered up with soap in the shower. Melanie's mind drifted to Chantal. She remembered meeting her for the first time at a gay nightclub two years ago. All eyes fell on Chantal. Melanie watched as her single friends made one failed attempt after another at getting to know Chantal better. Their corny "heard it before" lines amused Chantal but did not impress her. Melanie found success at the end of the night with a simple hello. Nneka drifted into Melanie's head. She was missing Nneka even though she had just seen her last night. Last night was special. Melanie smiled with the remembrance of it. She longed to have her near. Melanie closed her eyes and a fantasy began to float into view. The scent of bacon wafted into the bathroom before the fantasy had the opportunity to fully develop into a wet daydream. Melanie sped up her shower, got dressed, and headed to the kitchen where Karen and Chantal were talking.

"You made breakfast," Melanie said, giving a half smile.

"Yeah, I thought I would surprise you guys."

Karen was chomping on a piece of bacon. She placed toast that had grape jelly spread across the top of it into her mouth when the sound of the master bedroom door being opened was heard. The three women turned their heads towards the hall leading to the master bedroom. In walked Keith. He had on a blue seersucker pajama set. His eyes surveyed the scene. Upon the sight of the women eating breakfast, Keith raised his right hand to his face then rested his chin upon its palm. His elbow rested upon his left arm that was wrapped around the front of his body.

"I thought I smelled bacon when I woke up. What are you guys doing? You couldn't wait for my breakfast specialty?"

Chantal's face relaxed into a slump, "Oh, I'm sorry," she managed to say.

"Hey, no one said we couldn't enjoy two breakfasts. Eat up, Mel," Karen said.

"Oh, someone's making breakfast? Does that mean someone else is living here now?" Keith said slyly. He raised his right hand towards his blonde curly locks then scratched his temple with his index finger.

No one responded. Melanie gave Keith a look that he recognized as a plea to go easy.

"Well, hurry up. Do whatever it is that y'all are doing. I need to make my man his meal, and you know the good doctor does not like to wait."

Keith retreated to his bedroom.

Melanie and Karen proceeded to eat Chantal's unwanted breakfast. After eating, Karen opened the front door to retrieve the paper.

"I've been meaning to ask for a while. Why do you guys call his boyfriend 'the good doctor'?" Chantal asked Melanie.

Melanie replied with, "Because he is a good guy, and he's a doctor," she punctuated her response with an expression that said duh.

Chantal felt as though she had just tripped onto a stage and into a performance she knew nothing about. "Hey, baby. I am going to head on out. I got a bunch of errands I need to run. Can you give me some money?" she said abruptly.

Melanie knew she should say no but she didn't want to risk Chantal getting mad and going off with someone who would say yes.

"Sure. Going so soon?" Melanie asked with a concern expression on her face. Though she enjoyed Chantal's company she couldn't help but to feel freedom rolling in. The more time Chantal was away the more money Melanie kept in her wallet.

"Yeah, I gotta go. I need to get caught up on some things after my trip. I'll see you later tonight."

Melanie went into her bedroom, came back out, and handed her girlfriend a roll of bills. Chantal grabbed her overnight bag. She then kissed Melanie, and told Karen goodbye as she headed out the door. Melanie locked the door behind her.

Karen stood in the living room staring at Melanie with an I-know-what-you've-been-up-to look. Karen walked passed Melanie to the door and looked out the peephole. The hall was clear.

"You gave money away you don't have. Plus, you entertained two women in one night, huh? You ought to be ashamed of yourself, Mel."

"I went to happy hour with friends."

"What friends? What are their names?"

"One guy's name is Mike."

"Who's Mike? You don't know a Mike?"

Melanie smiled slyly. "Oh, yes I do?"

"What you messing with guys now?"

"Hey now," Melanie snapped back.

"Mmm, I'm suspicious."

"Mmm, whatever, Karen."

"Let it be known that I am not going to be lying to any of your women for you. So you better do some cleaning up because it's getting messy now that you have one of them spending the night."

"I got this. And stop acting like you're Mother Teresa or something."

"Okay, Ms. I-got-this. I never said I was Mother Teresa. Unlike you, I don't do things in the dark. All I am going to say is I hope your other one is not a gold-digger like this one. I don't know why you are so into Chantal. Yeah she's cute and all, but you two have nothing in common. She uses you because you let her. I'd hate to see where you end up if you had two gold-diggers on your hands. There has to be women out there who you're compatible with and is into art like you. I know you don't love Chantal. So why are you with her?"

Melanie looked squarely at her cousin. "You are killing me with your rambling and preaching. It's too early for all this talking. I've heard it before. It's redundant. I'm not interested in what you are saying so drop it." Melanie looked away and thought about Nneka.

Karen saw that her question struck a nerve with her cousin. "Hey forget what I said. Let's go get us some real breakfast before we start arguing over dumb stuff," she said.

"Now, that's the best thing you said all morning," Melanie said.

Karen smiled at her cousin and shook her head.

Later that day, Melanie and Karen walked up to the register to pay for their usual three games at the local bowling alley. It was packed with people. Shouts and screams were heard from strikes and gutter balls. Chantal, Keith, and the good doctor made their way to their usual number eleven lane. There was no need to rent shoes or use the highly-used bowling balls as they each had their own. Chantal even had her name inscribed in gold lettering on her red ball. It was a gift from Melanie. Melanie and Karen soon joined the group at the lane.

"It's really sad the three of you can never beat the two of us," the good doctor said as he punched in their information onto the scoreboard. "Well, really, the four of you will never beat the one of me. I should just be my own team," he continued as he chuckled to himself.

No one responded as it was the same rhetoric they'd heard a million times before. The good doctor always managed to say it as though it was the first time and never seemed to get tired of chuckling at his own comments.

Melanie saw the good doctor was about to press "enter" indicating that all players' names had been entered, including his own real name, Adam. She stopped him before his finger reached the enter button, "Wait, we have a visitor coming tonight," she said.

Everyone looked at Melanie puzzled.

"My friend, Mike, from work is coming."

"Your pretend friend from work, you mean," Karen said.

"No. He's real. You best believe that he's real," Melanie began to grin like the Cheshire Cat from the book *Alice's Adventures in Wonderland.*

Karen became suspicious. Melanie continued to grin.

"Okay, Mike it is," Adam punched in the name and hit enter. He stood up and stretched his long, tanned, and muscular arms above his buzzed-cut straight, black hair.

Melanie stood up and announced she was going to put in their order for food and drinks. Keith stated he would walk to the counter with her.

"So what's up with this Mike person?"

"Well, do you remember Big Mike from back in the day?" Melanie whispered even though they were no longer in earshot of the group.

"Yeah, I do," Keith whispered back.

"Well, we now work together. He started earlier this week. He's the one I've been hanging out with after work. We've been catching up."

"Oh my goodness, Karen is going to flip when she sees him."

"I know, that's why I've been keeping it a secret. I can't wait to see the expression on her face."

Melanie and Keith placed their order. They began to head back to the lane when Melanie felt someone staring at her. She looked around. Her eyes rested upon Nneka. She was on lane five with her mom, dad, and younger sister. Melanie's heart gave a strong thump. It was soon followed by a sense of worry that Chantal was only a few lanes away. Melanie wanted to walk over to Nneka, but her feet continued to move to her group. She turned her head away.

"You're up, Mel," Chantal said.

A shaky Melanie reached for her ball and wiped it down with a towel. She stepped up to her spot but could not focus. She released the ball. It was an instant gutter. A more delayed gutter ball followed the instant gutter ball. No spare.

"You have got to be kidding me, Melanie," Karen said in disbelief.

"I just need to warm up."

"So, Karen, isn't it weird how the past just kind of catches up with people at the oddest moments?" Keith said with the same Cheshire Cat grin that once graced Melanie's face.

"What are you talking about? Are you and Mel smoking the same stuff?"

"No, just saying. You never know when the past will come up and bite you in the ass."

Adam looked at Keith trying to figure out what was going on.

Chantal was up next to bowl. "Mel, if I break a nail you are going to have to give me some dead presidents to fix it."

Karen rolled her eyes after overhearing Chantal's comment. Chantal rolled the ball. She continued standing at her spot waiting to see the results of her roll. Melanie looked over at Nneka who appeared to be having a good time with her family. Two pins fell over.

"I hate this game," Chantal said.

Karen slid over to an empty chair next to Melanie.

"Don't look. There is a hot guy over to the back and left who keeps looking at me. Don't look."

Melanie didn't look. "Where's he at?"

"Okay, look slowly. See the woman with the red flowery blouse on?"

Melanie stretched her arms and looked over her shoulder. She saw the woman wearing the red flowery blouse. She also saw Mike standing next to her. Melanie smiled. "He *is* a hot guy," Melanie said with a smile.

"I know. He has been over there for a couple of minutes now. What should I do?"

"Go over and say hi. He's probably trying to figure out if you have a man around or not."

"Oh no. I could never do that. Desperate women do that."

"Well it looks like you don't have to."

"Why?"

"He's coming this way."

Karen froze. She shifted her body away from Mike so that she was facing the lanes.

Melanie stood up and said, "Hey, Mike, welcome to the party."

Karen mouthed the words, "That's Mike."

"This is my cousin, Keith, his partner, Adam, my girl Chantal," Melanie pointed to Chantal who was about to roll. "The one hiding here is my lovely cousin, Karen."

Keith's previous grin grew even larger.

"It's good seeing you again, Karen," Mike said.

"Is that my roomie?" Chantal said as she looked down the lanes towards lane five.

Melanie overheard Chantal and stiffened.

"What do you mean it's good to see me again?" Karen said as she turned to face Mike who was now sitting next to her.

Keith nudged Adam. Adam wrinkled his forehead trying to figure out what he was witnessing. It would soon be his turn to bowl but he could not decide if he should roll or stay to watch the mystery unfolding before him.

"That *is* my girl. Nneka!" Chantal shouted.

Nneka did not hear Chantal's call. She kept conversing with her mother.

Chantal rolled her ball quickly and ended up getting a spare.

"Yeah, baby, that's how you do it!" she shouted. She ran back to the group expecting high fives but instead saw Karen with a puzzled look on her face looking at Mike, Keith, and Adam watching the duo, and Melanie standing stiff like a statue in one of Kansas City's plethora of water fountains.

"Mel, I got a spare," Chantal said.

Melanie still in a daze looked through Chantal.

"Oh that's great, baby," She raised her hand and gave a limp high five.

"You guys are tripping. I'm going to run over and say hey to Nneka. I'll be right back."

"Maybe you remember me better with cake smeared on my face." Melanie heard Mike say to Karen. Melanie was so engrossed in watching Chantal walk over to Nneka that she missed Karen's stunned and embarrassed expression. Melanie then heard Keith laugh and say, "Bites you right there on the ass," as he pointed to his own rear end.

CHAPTER SIX

A week later Melanie used her key to enter Chantal and Nneka's apartment. "Anyone home?" She shouted. There was no response. She walked through the living room that had drawings from Nneka. There were also a couple of pictures of Melanie and Chantal together on the oak entertainment center.

Melanie walked to Chantal's room. Clothes were tossed about her bed. Stiletto heels littered the floor. Cylinders of mascara, compacts, and tubes of lipstick lay across her vanity. Melanie noted that it looked like chaos. She walked farther to the back of the apartment to Nneka's bedroom. One of Nneka's favorite quotes hung from one of her walls. Melanie transcribed it. She wrote it in calligraphy. It read: "If you knew how much work went into it, you wouldn't call it genius. —Michelangelo"

One of the bedroom's windows was open. The wind gently blew Nneka's white lace curtains. Her art supplies were neatly placed in containers next to an easel. Melanie wondered why they weren't downstairs in her rented studio. She turned around to head to the kitchen for a glass of water. Melanie pulled out her cell phone and dialed Chantal's number as she sipped the cool refreshment.

"Hey, baby," Chantal said.

"Hey, you. When you coming home?"

"My home or your home?"

"Your home."

"Not for a while. It looks like this shoot is going to be a long one. I probably won't be back until after ten or so."

Melanie heard keys chiming at the door. In walked Nneka with the drawing Melanie did of her a few weeks ago.

"Okay. Well, I just wanted to call and say that I love you," Melanie said as she looked intensely into Nneka's eyes.

"Ah that's sweet, baby. I haven't heard that in a long time. I love you too. I gotta run. I will talk with you later."

Chantal hung up.

"I love you with all of my heart and soul," Melanie said to Nneka.

"I can't tell Melanie. Especially when you are whipping up a good time with Chantal and your family," Nneka said sternly. "I can't do this anymore," she said in a softer tone.

Melanie felt Nneka distancing herself emotionally from her.

"I know."

"I want you to leave now."

"But I don't want to leave."

"And I don't want you to stay." Nneka fought back tears. She looked over at the pictures of Melanie and Chantal. She saw how they physically seemed to blend into one another, differing skin tone but same high attractiveness.

"I'm not the cover girl you want to be with. So why don't you just leave me alone."

"You are beautiful. You are everything I dream of."

"And that's where it is, in your head, in your dream world away from others to see." Nneka crossed her arms tightly across her waist. "Just go be in reality with your girl and leave me alone." Tears flowed from her eyes. The pain of the realization of her nowhere relationship burned in her chest. Denial tried to cloak the pain but it had already gotten a hold of Nneka's aching heart.

Melanie stepped forward to embrace Nneka. Nneka shifted quickly away and looked at Melanie with an icy coldness that sent shivers down Melanie's spine. Melanie walked to the door. Her gut told her to come clean to Chantal. It told her to make a commitment and declare her love for Nneka to everyone. But the pride of having the beautiful Chantal on her arm kept her anchored. Melanie turned the knob of the apartment's front door. Her gut yelled to her she was making a mistake. She opened the door. Her gut screamed to stop. She walked through the door.

CHAPTER SEVEN

The following evening Melanie and Mike were playing a video game. Karen seasoned and placed chicken wings in the oven. She then started working on a dip for chips and vegetables.

Mike pushed the pause button on his controller. "Give me a second," he said to Melanie. Melanie slouched back into the couch. Mike walked into the kitchen. "Karen, whatever you are whipping up in here smells great."

Melanie sarcastically mouthed the same words that had just been spoken by Mike.

Karen blushed. "Thanks. Just felt like doing something a little different tonight. We usually eat out."

"Well, is there anything I can help you with?"

"Sure, how about helping clean the celery and carrots."

"I'm on it."

Melanie scrunched her face. "Hey what about the game?" she shouted.

"It can wait," Mike said, "I'm helping out in the kitchen."

Melanie rolled her eyes. She stood up and walked to the balcony door. She saw Chantal's car pulling into a parking spot. A few minutes later she heard keys jingling at the door. Melanie walked over to give Chantal a hug. Instead Chantal shoved an overnight bag into Melanie's arms.

"Thanks, baby," Chantal said as she rushed by Melanie to get to the bedroom.

Melanie pursed her lips and sighed. She placed her left hand on the door to close it when she felt a give. She turned around and saw Keith and Adam. Keith was carrying a slow cooker filled with barbeque meatballs. Adam carried a chilled bowl of potato salad.

"We need to do this more often. Home cooked meals," Adam said.

"I agree," Karen said from the kitchen.

Keith walked to Karen's voice.

"Looks like you two are getting cozy," Keith said to Karen and Mike.

Mike looked at Karen and gave a warm smile.

"I guess you can say that," Karen said.

"Oh no, no, no we are not going to be playing this," Adam said as he looked at the frozen screen of the video game. "Is this saved?"

"Yeah, you can go ahead and shut it off," Melanie said glumly, still holding Chantal's overnight bag. Melanie heard the shower turn on, which was followed by the closing of the bathroom door. She walked to her bedroom and placed Chantal's bag on the bed. On her way back she stopped at the hall closet, opened it, and pulled down the game Scene It.

"You sure are on the gloomy side tonight," Adam said as Melanie reentered the living room.

"She has been like that all day. Not sure what's going on," Karen said.

A freshly showered Chantal came out from the bathroom. She had on a pair of pink pajama shorts and a matching tank top. Her lips had a soft shine from the clear gloss she glided across them.

"The food smells great. Can't wait to dig in," Chantal said.

"Everything should be done in a few minutes," Karen said.

"Melanie, can I talk to you for a minute?" Chantal asked.

"Sure." Melanie placed the game on the coffee table and followed Chantal to the bedroom.

Chantal closed the door.

"What's this about?" Melanie asked.

"This is about you and Nneka."

"What?" Melanie said breathlessly.

"Nneka told me everything as she packed up her stuff and left. I knew something was going on with you, but I wouldn't have thought in a million years that it was Nneka. Nneka is so blah. She's nothing more than a nerdy, frumpy artist. How could you go from this to that?" Chantal motioned her hands as if presenting herself. She then shifted her hands towards an emptiness that represented Nneka. "Don't get me wrong she's my girl and all, but come on."

Melanie felt herself getting defensive with every negative word Chantal released about Nneka.

Chantal paused for a moment to collect her thoughts and composure. She continued, "Well, in the end. You came to your senses. You chose me so that's all that matters. I forgive you, but I won't forget. I'm sure I can think of ways you can make it up to me. Ways you can begin to rebuild your image, strengthen my trust in you."

This is the person I chose to be with. The reality of the situation made Melanie feel like she had just got the wind punched out of her by a heavy weight champ. The room went black, her heart sunk, she was motionless. *What in the world did I do?* Melanie thought. *Why in the hell am I with this woman?* A puzzled look came upon Melanie's face. *Where is my Nneka?* Melanie wondered.

"Are you listening to me?" Chantal asked.

Melanie said, "Yes."

Chantal responded as if reading Melanie's mind. "Nneka moved to a place she didn't want me to disclose to you. Now let's stop all this mopping around. It's depressing me. Go get washed up so we can get our grub on."

Chantal took a step towards the door then turned around and said, "Remember, you were nothing before you met me. You need me." With that said Chantal left the room and closed the door behind her.

Melanie sat on her bed and leaned forward with her hands clasped together. She looked over at her sketchpad leaning against a wall. Tears filled her eyes. The Billie Holiday song "Crazy He Calls Me" played in her head. Melanie sung her own lyrics in a soft tone to the tune as she choked back tears. "The difficult I did. The impossible will never be."

Melanie wiped her face as best she could. She then stood up to walk out the bedroom door and into the void that would be her life. Her cell phone rang when her hand touched the door knob. She walked over to her dresser to pick it up. She saw the picture of a sunrise she had taken with Nneka show up on the screen. Without missing a beat, Melanie hit the answer button.

"Hello," she said as if she was taking her last breath. The pleasant sound of Nneka's voice flowed through the phone into Melanie's ears to melt her heart. Melanie fell back onto her bed; her cheeks were soon smothered in tears. It was as if she was being washed from the heavens with a second chance. Melanie managed to say in between sobs, "Oh my goodness, Nneka, I love you. You are the one for me. Where are you?" Melanie quickly retrieved a piece of paper and a pen then jotted down the address. "I am on my way now. I have to do something first. But I will see you soon. I love you." Melanie hung up the phone. She raised her head towards the ceiling, kissed the side of her right index finger, and said thank you. Melanie pushed her shoulders back and walked through her bedroom door. She no longer felt anchored; she was on her way to set her life straight. She was on her way to the sweetness.

HALLOWED

ADRIANNA

CHAPTER ONE

A dragonfly flew through a neighborhood in Lincoln, Nebraska on a warm spring day. It zipped past a tan toy poodle barking in a backyard, through the legs of a gas grill, and up to a screen of a closed bedroom window where it rested.

Adrianna secured tape to a cardboard box. She stood up, raised her arms above her head, closed her beautifully slanted eyes, and stretched her slender, golden bronze body. Adrianna relaxed and opened her eyes. She saw the dragonfly on her screen. She walked over to the window to get a closer look at it. Adrianna took in its green iridescent body and white, semi-translucent wings. She then turned her attention away to her walk-in bedroom closet. She walked inside and saw the last items hanging, her mother's traditional Chinese dresses. They hadn't been moved since her death thirteen years ago when Adrianna was ten.

"Here we go, Mom. A new home. A new life," Adrianna said aloud as if her mother was standing by her side. One by one, Adrianna removed each dress with gentle movements. She then placed them in a beige garment bag. Once all the dresses were in, she placed the bag in the middle of her bare bedroom. With her hands on her hips, she surveyed the room. *Twenty-three years and it ends here,* she thought.

"Hey, baby. Are you ready to eat?"

Adrianna turned around and saw her boyfriend, Thaddeus, standing in the door way. He had on a pair of brown leather slip-on loafers, khaki pants, and a peach-colored polo shirt that made his brown skin glow. His luminous brown eyes radiated love for Adrianna.

"Yeah, I can feel my tummy begin to rumble." Adrianna placed her left hand over her abdomen. "What did my dad cook up? It smells good but I can't tell what it is."

"That's probably because it is a mixture of things. He started out making a beef stew from one of your mother's recipes but it didn't turn out right. So then he went to plan B and made spaghetti with spicy Italian sausage meatballs … with the help of Aunt Serena, of course."

Adrianna gave a slight smile with the thought of her father attempting to make her mother's scrumptious beef stew.

"Yeah, of course. Spaghetti sounds good," Adrianna said. She walked towards Thaddeus who embraced her with his slight muscular arms once she had gotten close enough.

"I love you," he whispered.

"I love you too," she whispered back.

"Heavenly Father, we thank you for the bounty we are about to receive. We thank you for all the blessings you have given us and for the challenges you have brought us through. We ask you look over my daughter and Thaddeus as they embark on a new chapter in their lives. Please fill their new home with your loving spirit. With you, Lord, we know that all things are possible. Amen."

"Amen," Adrianna, Serena, and Thaddeus said in unison.

"Auntie and Dad, this looks and smells great," Adrianna said as her father, Darren, placed the bowls and plates around the table.

"Thank you," Serena and Darren said together. "We are just happy to be able to share a meal before you two take off to faraway Omaha," Serena continued.

Thaddeus laughed quietly "Yeah, all the way to Omaha. Why does everyone keep referring to it as some faraway place? It's only about an hour drive from here," he said.

"Because when people move to Omaha they rarely come back to visit. Then they usually spring off to some other city in another state. It's like a springboard city," Darren said as his brown hand and fingers twirled his fork in the bowl of pasta that sat in front of him.

Serena nodded in agreement.

Adrianna took a small bite of her garlic bread then said, "We will come back to visit."

"Really?" Darren said, looking his daughter in her eyes.

"Yeah, I'll be back, Dad," she said sincerely.

CHAPTER TWO

Adrianna sat quietly in Thaddeus's grey car. Thaddeus maneuvered the sedan onto the highway heading east towards Omaha. They had boxes and piles of clothes in the backseat that came up to just below Thaddeus's view out the rearview mirror. Thaddeus began to move faster than the speed limit.

"Slow down a bit," Adrianna said.

"Sorry, baby. I'm just excited to get us to *our* home." Thaddeus took his right hand and gave Adrianna's left hand a soft squeeze before returning it to the steering wheel. "Our life together is beginning at this moment. Can you believe it? A few years ago, we met at the open mic night at the coffee shop. You allowed me the pleasure," Thaddeus placed his right hand over his chest, "of taking you out on our first date. A picnic at your favorite park."

Adrianna smiled at the memory. She remembered how comfortable she was when they first met. Everything just seemed to fall into place. It was as if they had rehearsed the moment numerous times in a previous life. "It was a nice date," she said as she glanced at him seeing the farmland rolling by on the other side of the car from her peripheral vision. She wondered why this moment was not feeling as well rehearsed as their past moments together.

Thaddeus continued on about how excited he was for them to be moving into their new home together. He proudly talked about his ability to encourage their agent to negotiate a deal he could brag to his colleagues, fellow financial analysts, at work about. Thaddeus also mentioned how happy he was about his commute being reduced by over an hour by not having to go between Omaha and Lincoln any longer.

Adrianna continued to sit quietly, looking out of her window saying the occasional me too, yup, and awesome.

An hour and a half later, they pulled up to their new corner lot home. The agent described it as a charming Craftsman. Thaddeus liked the spaciousness of the home and the huge backyard. Adrianna liked the maroon shutters that framed the windows and how it contrasted with the grey siding. Thaddeus parked the car behind the U-haul truck he and his friends had unloaded earlier in the day.

Adrianna and Thaddeus removed some of the items from the backseat of his car and continued the process of moving their belongings into the house. Before long, Adrianna retrieved the last items that included the garment bag and cassette tapes that were in a big, pink gift bag with a green bow stapled to the front. There was nothing further for Thaddeus to retrieve. They both turned around and walked up to the front door.

Thaddeus held Adrianna back before she walked into the house. He took the bags from her and placed them inside the home. He looked at her and said, "Let's do this the proper way." He lifted her up, her back rested against his left arm as her legs dangled over his right arm. She placed her right arm around his neck. They kissed as Thaddeus carried her over the threshold. The feeling of joy came over Thaddeus. At the same time as Thaddeus closed the door behind them, the feeling of doom came over Adrianna.

CHAPTER THREE

Adrianna and Molly, her pregnant best friend, strolled the sidewalks in Omaha's art and entertainment district, The Old Market. The wind picked up. The scent of Chanel No. 5 lifted from Adrianna's wrists and swirled around in the breeze. The wind blew Molly's straight black hair across the left side of her rosy cheeks and sunglasses. She removed the strands from her face with her hand. Her wedding ring sparkled in the sunlight with her movement. The wind died down.

"This is awesome. We both left sleepy Lincoln for Omaha. We both have husbands who work for the same company. And soon, we'll both have babies in our bellies," Molly said as she sparkled with excitement.

"Well, it could be said Omaha is just as sleepy as Lincoln," Adrianna replied flatly.

"Well, Omaha has taller buildings."

"True. Why do you keep referring to Thaddeus as my husband?"

"Uh, because it's inevitable. I'm surprised he hasn't popped the question yet. And when he does, babies are sure to follow. We can raise our kids together. They'll be best friends just like us," Molly said.

Adrianna's heart filled with warmth with the thought of her future child having as good a friend as Molly. She smiled. Molly opened her mouth and let out a cloud of air that rose to her nose. She could smell the onions from the omelet she devoured for breakfast. Molly began to rummage through her purse for a piece of gum.

"Well, Thaddeus proposed to me."

Molly inhaled deeply almost choking on her gum. "What? When? Where's the ring?" Molly shrieked, which made Adrianna laugh.

"Finally! A little laughter. You've been so down all day today. I've been trying to figure it out. Well, why were you so down? This is supposed to be a girls' day of fun. It doesn't get any better than to have free reign of Thaddeus's credit card to buy furnishings for your house. Well, go on. Tell me the details," Molly said anxiously.

"First, I told him I had to think about it. Think about what it means."

A baffled look came across Molly's face. "Think about what it means. Girl, you lost me."

"I don't know. I'm just not ready. When I figure it out I'll let you know."

"Adrianna, you seem so cheerless when you're supposed to be cheerful."

"I'm confused."

"Confused about what?"

Adrianna shrugged her shoulders. "I don't know. That's why I'm confused." The smile that once graced her face was slowly being replaced by her previously sullen expression.

Molly stopped walking. Adrianna walked a couple of steps then turned around to see why Molly stopped. Molly walked up to Adrianna and lifted her sunglasses to the top of her head. She gently removed Adrianna's sunglasses. Adrianna turned away.

"What's wrong, Adrianna?"

"I don't know. I wish I knew," Adrianna said, sniffing back a runny rose.

"Aren't you happy to be with Thaddeus?"

"Of course I am."

"Do you love him?"

"With all of my heart."

"Then what is it?"

Adrianna looked at the French script lettering on the window of an antique store.

"I don't know." Adrianna reached for her sunglasses. Molly handed them over.

"How about we take a look in this store," Adrianna said as she placed her sunglasses back on.

A concerned Molly dropped the subject. She wrapped her left arm around Adrianna's shoulders, giving her a delicate kiss on her cheek and said, "Sure."

Maria's "Intoxicating" was playing from Adrianna's car's stereo as she drove home from her outing with Molly. She was moving at the speed limit on the highway when she saw the brake lights from the cars ahead of her come on. Adrianna saw that the speed was going to drop to a crawl. She looked ahead to see if she could see an exit off. There was none. She too began to slow to a crawl.

"Great," she said to herself when the crawl turned into a stop and slow-go. "Construction season sucks," she said to herself.

Adrianna glanced back at her new purchases of green, blue, and brown accent pieces. She began to imagine them in the living room furnished with the new heather grey sectional and matching chair she had ordered from the furniture store. Adrianna couldn't wait to see the expression on Thaddeus's face when he saw it for the first time.

Adrianna began to sing along with the song on the radio, "'Cause you're so intoxicating, I'm loving everything you do, constantly you've got me craving, I can't get enough of you," she sang passionately with Thaddeus in mind. Thoughts of Thaddeus began to relax her. Soon, as it often did at relaxed moments like this, she began remembering her father's philandering ways during her childhood and teenage years, and the devastating effects it had on her. Adrianna's body stiffened.

Adrianna's focus turned back to the road ahead of her when she saw lights flashing from emergency vehicles on the left side of the highway. Adrianna turned off the music. Her hands began to get clammy. Her breathing slowed. The traffic continued at the stop and slow-go pace. Her car inched closer to the lights. Adrianna's body was hollow. Her chest began to vibrate with the increasing quick thumps of her heartbeat.

Adrianna's eyes widened when she got close enough to see an overturned black car and silver SUV in a ditch. She also saw a white car with Missouri plates that had its front end pushed in like a decrepit accordion. Adrianna's body turned numb when she saw the vehicle's passenger side door open and a white sheet covering a body. She watched as the emergency personnel heaved the back right door open. A policeman reached in and removed a hysterical toddler from the vehicle. The officer tried to place the little girl in the hands of an emergency medical technician but she kept reaching for the body underneath the white sheet. Adrianna could see the girl mouthing the word mommy over and over again.

Adrianna slipped into a daze. In her mind, she saw herself walking cautiously to the white sheet that blanketed one of the accident's victims. She stopped walking when she was within inches of the deceased person. She then kneeled down. With trembling hands, she slowly pulled the sheet back and saw her mother, eyes closed lying on the hot pavement with blood trickling from her nose. Warm tears rolled down Adrianna's cheeks. The cries of the toddler cut through her ears. She turned and saw her ten-year-old self standing behind her. It was her age when her mother passed away in a car accident. Gradually, everything around them turned silent and black.

"Is my mommy dead?" her ten-year-old self asked in a somber tone.

Adrianna nodded her head.

"Who's going to take care of me?" her ten-year-old self asked.

Adrianna looked down, "I don't know," she replied in a shaky whisper.

A knock on Adrianna's car window shook her back to the present moment. It was an officer. Adrianna looked at him with dazed eyes. She heard him say, "Please keep moving, miss." Adrianna nodded a little. She turned her head forward to see the car in front of her was about twenty-five yards up the highway from her.

Later that evening, Adrianna sat on her bed in the dimly lit master bedroom as she listened to the news of the accident on her television. The female news anchor recapped what had happened: a three-vehicle collision on I-480 east, one dead, two in critical condition, and a child who was treated and released. Adrianna turned the television off. She looked at the clock. It read 8:00 p.m. Thaddeus was working late. She wished he was home with her at that moment. She needed him. She walked to her closet, retrieved the large pink gift bag. She removed a cassette tape, walked over to the stereo, placed it in, and pressed play. Adrianna lowered herself to the floor and began to listen to an entry of her mother's audio diaries.

A half hour later, Adrianna heard the front door open and close. Adrianna shot up from the floor. She rushed to Thaddeus who immediately held her tight.

"What's wrong, baby?" Thaddeus asked in a worried tone.

"I miss my mom," Adrianna replied through tears as her body shook.

Thaddeus closed his eyes and held her tighter.

CHAPTER FOUR

The following morning a somber Adrianna made waffles, eggs, and bacon for herself and Thaddeus. She poured coffee in a cup for him. For herself, she poured hot water over an Earl Grey tea bag. A sleepy Thaddeus dragged his feet into the kitchen.

"Good morning," he said then planted a kiss on Adrianna's cheek. "Smells great in here."

"Thanks, I figured it's the least I could do given that you listened—"

Thaddeus interrupted Adrianna. "We are a team. There is no such thing as paybacks. Now come sit down with me and enjoy this meal you made for us."

Adrianna gave a frail smile and sat next to Thaddeus.

Later that morning, Thaddeus said, "Are you sure you don't want me to go with you?" as he kneeled down beside the driver's side door with Adrianna sitting at the wheel.

"I'm sure. I need to do this alone."

"Okay, well call me if you need anything."

"I will."

They kissed.

Adrianna backed out of the driveway and headed to her father's home in Lincoln.

Thoughts of all she wanted to say floated through her head during the drive. She wondered how he was going to respond. Though she had the power of Thaddeus's encouragement and support coursing through her, she wondered if she would have the strength to release what she had been holding inside for thirteen years.

Adrianna pulled up to the curb of her childhood home. She sat for a moment remembering the day her mother, Bic, caught her father cheating on her with Bic's best friend, Mia. Adrianna also remembered the scores of women, which included Mia, who came in and out of the house after Bic had died.

She clasped her hands together and raised them to her forehead. "You can do this," she said to herself.

"Adrianna!"

Adrianna raised her head to see her Aunt Serena standing in the doorway.

"Girl, I thought that was you. Why are you sitting in your car? Come inside," Serena yelled.

A relief that her aunt was at the house washed over Adrianna. She quickly climbed out of the car and walked into the house.

The scent of fresh paint greeted Adrianna at the doorway. She looked over her aunt who had a white and black paisley print scarf wrapped around her head and tied in the back. Serena had on black cotton shorts and a blue T-shirt. Adrianna also saw camel-colored paint on her arms and legs.

"You're painting?"

"Yeah, started helping your father paint your old bedroom," Serena replied as she walked to the kitchen. Mahalia Jackson's soulful rendition of "God Will Take Care of You" was playing on a small radio that was on top of one of the countertops.

"Oh really?" Adrianna said, following her into the kitchen.

Serena opened the freezer door, took out two corndogs. "You want one?"

"No thanks, I'm good. I had breakfast. So what are you guys doing with my old room?"

"We're turning it into a meditation room."

"Meditation room, huh. How long you think this born again Christian thing is going to last?" Adrianna asked.

"For as long as it makes him feel full and happy. You know, it might do you some good to attend service with him some time."

"Hmm. Where is he anyway?"

Serena walked over to the counter, wrapped the corndogs in a paper towel, and then placed them in the microwave. "At church. They have an annual conference going on right now."

"How long will that take?" Adrianna leaned her body against one of the kitchen's walls.

"He won't be back until around nine or ten tonight."

Adrianna looked down. Disappointment swept across her face. "I wanted to talk to him."

Serena put one hand on her hip as she looked at her niece. "I can tell. May I ask what it is you want to talk to him about?"

"I want to talk about my mom, all the women, if he loved my mom … if he loves me." Adrianna said as she looked down at the floor.

"Adrianna, look at me."

Adrianna raised her eyes to her aunt though her head still hung low.

"Yes, he loved your mother. The women were distractions. Yes, he loved and loves you."

The microwave beeped. Serena took the corndogs out, placed them on a plate, and sat down at the kitchen table. Adrianna walked over to the table and sat with her.

"How do you know?" Adrianna said, peering deep into her aunt's brown eyes.

Serena kept the eye contact and said, "Because I am his big sister, and I've been knowing the man for forty plus years."

Adrianna inhaled deeply then released a sigh. "Then why did he do what he did to my mom. Why did he hurt her?"

Serena broke eye contact with Adrianna. Serena slouched as her eyes moved down and to the left. "Because our father cheated on our mother. Darren and I saw him with another woman one day after school when we were in junior high. We told Mama and when confronted, Daddy denied it and called us liars. After that he threatened to send us off to a children's home if we ever said anything again. Daddy kept seeing that woman *and* other women. Mama knew but she just went about her business as if nothing was happening. Darren loved Mama but he began to lose respect for her as time went on, and the women continued to come and go. It didn't make sense to him why she allowed him to treat her the way he did. I, on the other hand, knew how hard it would be for her and us if she tried to make it on her own. I knew she figured she just wasn't that strong of a person to make that sort of change. So, she stayed."

Adrianna was dumbfounded by the similarities. She wrinkled her forehead and said, "I never knew that."

Serena raised her eyebrows and sat up straight. She took a bite out of one of the corndogs and said, "It isn't exactly a happy memory," with her mouth partially full.

"Yeah, it's not," Adrianna said knowingly while looking down.

"Your father loved your mother deeply." Serena paused for a moment. She took her right hand and lifted Adrianna's chin up tenderly and looked into her eyes. She continued, "The feelings he had for her scared and confused him. He just didn't know how to express it."

Adrianna felt a connection was being made in a slow manner. She did not fully understand her father's decisions but she felt a little lighter after learning more about Darren's past. Adrianna wrapped her arms around her aunt and said, "Thank you, Auntie."

CHAPTER FIVE

The following week, Adrianna and Darren walked hand in hand through the cemetery where Bic was laid to rest. Adrianna listened to the birds chirping and the leaves rustling in the wind above her. The afternoon sun shined down on the plethora of pink, orange, red, and purple flowers placed mindfully throughout the cemetery. It also shined on the bouquet of orange roses, white daisies, and a tan linen bag that Darren carried.

Adrianna felt her mother's comforting presence. She also felt the freshness of moving forward and embracing her own future.

Adrianna and Darren reached Bic's gravesite. Adrianna read the words that were engraved into Bic's headstone to herself: *Memories Will Carry Us Through, As the Angels Have Carried You*

Darren released Adrianna's hand then kneeled down to the ground. He placed the flowers beside the stone, reached into the linen bag, and removed two pairs of shears from the bag. He handed a pair to Adrianna. She took the shears but continued to stand as she watched Darren cut the grass around the stone. It was as if he had done this many times before.

Adrianna smiled. She then kneeled down to the ground and began trimming the grass with her father.

"I've always told you that all men are not like me," Darren said without looking at his daughter.

Adrianna nodded as she continued trimming. She said, "I remember."

"Thaddeus is a good man. You would be a fool to let him get away over things that have nothing to do with him or you. He's not a dog like your pops."

Adrianna stopped trimming. She placed her hands on her lap. Adrianna looked at the side of her father's face and said, "You're human, Dad, and I love you."

Darren stopped trimming. He remained in the kneeling position motionless.

"Dad," Adrianna said trying to figure out what was happening.

Adrianna reached her right hand out to touch Darren's shoulder when he lifted his watery eyes towards his daughter. He held his arms out to her. They embraced. Adrianna felt the presence of her mother as she melted into the sweetness of her father's hug. Adrianna closed her eyes. Darren held his daughter close. For the first time, Adrianna felt her once hollow body fill with love. It was a love that radiated between her and her father.

CHAPTER SIX

"I wish I could stay for the big moment," Molly said as she placed white candles on the stairs of Adrianna and Thaddeus's home.

Adrianna was making sure all of the sage green pillows were nicely arranged on the newly delivered heather grey sofa and chair.

"I will be sure to tell you every little detail … well not *every* detail." Adrianna winked. She then walked into the kitchen to remove chocolate-covered strawberries from the refrigerator. Molly joined her in the kitchen. Adrianna leaned against the kitchen island, and Molly leaned against the counter across from her.

"So tonight is the night," Molly said with a grin.

"Hopefully, I will be on my way to being a Mrs."

"Oh so you're not going to be a feminist? You're going for the Mrs., huh?"

"Yeah, why not? I like the sound of it. It's like we are one."

"Right on. Cheers to a new beginning," Molly said as she held up an imaginary wine glass.

Adrianna too held up her invisible glass. "Cheers to new beginnings and new friendships," Adrianna rubbed Molly's belly then her own.

Molly's jaw dropped towards the ground along with her imaginary glass. "Oh my God, are you pregnant?"

Adrianna waved her hand no. "Not yet."

"Oh my word, you can't do that to a pregnant woman." Molly placed her hand over her rapidly beating heart. "Where's the ring?"

"Right here." Adrianna walked out of the room and came back with a small black velvet box.

"I can't wait to see it."

"Me too. I didn't even give the poor guy the chance to open the box before I started to freak out."

"I could just about imagine his face. Finally worked up the nerves to ask and then you give him the unexpected answer of no."

"Yeah it was a bit much. But now it will be different. Can you grab the champagne and flutes while I carry this tray of strawberries up to the bedroom?"

"Absolutely."

The two friends left the kitchen and made their way to the master bedroom.

Later that evening, Thaddeus came home to a candlelit entryway and stairs. The scent of vanilla filled the air.

Adrianna watched him enter from the top of the stairs. She was dressed in a white silk negligee. Thaddeus looked up and saw her at the top of the stairs. He started to say something but Adrianna pointed to an item on the entryway table. He saw a notecard. He held it to a candle's light and read: *Please ask me again.*

Thaddeus's heart filled with joy. He started to sprint up the stairs to Adrianna but he thought it better not to in case he knocked down one of the candles. Instead he took off his jacket and coolly placed it in the hall closet. He turned his attention to the candle on the entryway table. He blew it out. He began to ascend the stairs.

At the third step he lifted a candle and blew it out. Adrianna's heart started to beat rapidly with anticipation. Thaddeus reached the fifth step, lifted another candle and blew it out. His heart rate matched Adrianna's. He reached the ninth step, lifted the candle and blew it out. He reached the top step and saw the ring box. He lifted the box in one hand and the last candle with the other. He then walked over to his girlfriend. Thaddeus got down on one knee, placed the candle down, and opened the box. Adrianna saw the sparkle of a diamond ring in the candlelight.

"Yes," she whispered in a choked-up voice before Thaddeus could say anything.

Thaddeus held up his right index finger, indicating Adrianna to wait.

He cleared his throat and asked, "Adrianna, will you do me the honor of marrying me?"

"Yes, Thaddeus. Yes, I will." Adrianna couldn't get the words out quick enough.

Thaddeus slid the ring onto Adrianna's finger. He blew the last candle out stood up and kissed his fiancée.

EXPOSED

NICOLE

CHAPTER ONE

The scent of fresh baked ziti filled the air in Nicole's parents' kitchen. A window was cracked open above the sink allowing the cool and crisp Detroit, Michigan air in. The low hum of traffic could be heard from the kitchen.

Nicole's brown hands were working well together. Her left hand held a stack of fresh basil leaves in place on a wooden cutting board, while her right hand retrieved more leaves to add to the heap. She meticulously began to roll the stack once all the leaves were in place. Air was pressed out from between the leaves as the pressure from the rolling increased. The rolling stopped and the last bit of air was released. Nicole then picked up her stepmother's, Ms. Anne's, chef's knife and began slicing the roll. Nicole soon laid the knife down then fluffed the sliced leaves. She closed her eyes when the refreshing scent of the basil reached her nose. She inhaled deeply, allowing the aroma to awaken her senses. Nicole opened her eyes. She leaned forward as she lifted the leaves from the cutting board and sprinkled them on top of the baked ziti that sat on a trivet. As if on cue, the garlic bread that was in the oven made its presence known with its robust buttery fragrance. Nicole removed it from the oven and placed it on top of the stove. Her family's dinner was ready.

"Honey, I just love it when you do cute things like this. They look like little green ribbons or something," Ms. Anne said. She admired the slice of decorated ziti Nicole placed on her plate.

"Thanks, Mom. It's a technique called chiffonade," Nicole replied.

"It looks as fancy as it sounds," Malcolm, Nicole's younger stepbrother, said.

Nicole looked into Malcolm's oblique shaped eyes and smiled. She then placed the remaining food on the dinner table close to her father.

"I taught you well," Marshal, Nicole's father, said with a wink.

Nicole remembered her father's lesson: meat near him, followed by the bread, please keep the veggies out of sight.

Nicole then took her place, across from Malcolm. The family began digging into their meal.

"When do finals start?" Ms. Anne asked Nicole.

"In three months. Thank goodness. I am so tired of school. I just want to get this thing done and over with so I can have my life back. Senior year is the worst year because that's where all of the higher level courses are."

"Well, I am proud of you, Nicole," Marshal said before taking a sip of water. "I couldn't have asked for a better daughter. Honor student in high school and about to be a graduate from the U of M," he continued after the water made its way down his throat.

"What's the name of your degree again so I can tell my friends at the convention?" Malcolm asked.

Nicole held her right hand over her mouth as she finished chewing the garlic bread. "Bachelor of business administration," she replied.

Ms. Anne looked at Nicole and said, "Then after that she's going back to school to learn culinary arts."

"Then open up a bakery," Marshal said.

"Where I can help sale cupcakes with my charm," Malcolm finished the list of goals the family had spoken about many times before.

"Whoa, one thing at a time. Gotta make it through finals first," Nicole said.

Ms. Anne bit into her salad then said, "Are you still okay with us throwing you some sort of graduation party?"

"Oh yeah, that'll be fine. I just want it to be small though. Just friends and family, the people who I am close to."

"You were closed to Crystal. Too bad she won't be there," Malcolm blurted out of nowhere.

Ms. Anne nudged Malcolm under the table with her foot to his.

"What?" he said to his mother, "Everyone knows how much Nicole liked, maybe even loved Crystal. She moved to Kansas City with Jerome, so that means she won't be here."

Nicole's mind wondered to the last memory of Crystal, her first crush. From her second-floor bedroom window, Nicole watched Crystal move. She watched Crystal place her belongings into the car of her drug dealing boyfriend, Jerome. Nicole remembered the desire that Crystal had shared with her. Crystal stated she wanted to be a mother and live in a Missouri suburb one day. Crystal hoped that The Show Me state would show her how good life could be. Nicole hoped Crystal's fantasy had come true. She hoped that Crystal was able to find the happiness that she had longed for and deserved. Nicole missed Crystal and dreamed one day she would see her again.

"Who knows, maybe I will see her again," Nicole said out loud what she was thinking.

God I hope not, Marshal thought.

"If you saw her again, then maybe you two will end up together," Malcolm said. "But then again, I don't know if two people can fit in your little apartment."

"My studio can fit two people."

"It would be a cozy fit," Ms. Anne said. "Did you ever take my advice and get some art up on your bare walls. They have some nice pictures at Jasmine's Beauty Mart."

Nicole smiled then said, "No, I haven't made it out there yet. I'll probably try and make it out tomorrow." She sat back in her chair as she remembered trips to the beauty store with Crystal. Nicole enjoyed watching her shop for the things that highlighted the attractiveness that God had given her naturally. Nicole said, "Black beauty supply stores are great. They are the only place where you can get all things that make us unique. Products for our kinky and curly hair, cocoa butter, weaves, picks, and du-rags. On your way to the register, be sure to pick up a picture of black Jesus, MLK, and Malcolm X."

The family laughed at Nicole's last remark.

"I used to like going there with Crystal," Nicole said with dreamy eyes.

Marshal wanted the conversation to change immediately. He asked a question he already knew the answer to, "Baby, when are you and Malcolm heading to the convention?"

Ms. Anne looked puzzled, "Uh, you know that the National Down Syndrome Annual Convention is a few months from now in July. You and I registered online together last week for NDSC."

"Yeah, yeah that's right, I just couldn't remember. Are you looking forward to going, Malcolm?"

"Yup, you know I am. Now that I am an old-timer, I get to show the little ones around."

"Old-timer, huh? Boy, you're only twenty. That would make me and Dad ancient."

Malcolm, Ms. Anne, and Marshal chuckled. Marshal looked at Nicole from the corner of his eyes. He saw her chuckling as well, but couldn't tell if it was in reaction to his wife's comments or to some thought of Crystal.

CHAPTER TWO

Nicole woke up in her apartment the following day. She was happy that the day was Saturday, which meant there was no class for her to go running off to. She had the entire day to do as she pleased, though she knew that one of those things should include at least two hours of study time. That, she decided, she would do at night.

Nicole washed up, got dressed in a black and white men's sweat suit with matching sneakers, ate breakfast, and headed out the door. She looked herself over in a mirror that hung in the hallway as she waited for the elevator. Nicole admired her light Caesar haircut. She had her father's skills with the razor to thank for that. She then turned her head side to side, making sure there were no pimples popping up on her smooth skin. The hall light cast a slight shadow on her lower cheeks as it hit her high cheekbones. The elevator bell beeped a few times, indicating its arrival. Nicole rode the elevator down five floors to the street level. She walked up to her used cashmere-colored Cadillac DeVille. It was a car she was proud of. The acquisition of the vehicle was the result of her hard work at her job in a check-processing unit at a bank.

Nicole drove her car up to a carwash attendant. She rolled her window down.

"What can I help you with today?" the attendant asked.

"I want the whole thing cleaned out," Nicole replied as she waved her hands in the car as if she were washing it herself with magical powers.

"Okay. We have a couple of packages for that," he replied.

The man went over the options with Nicole. She chose the package she wanted then left her car in the attendant's care. Nicole made her way into the store to pay and wait for her vehicle. She sat on a purple and red-checkered chair that was framed with oak wood. Nicole rested her elbows on her knees as she looked down at the blue, tiled floor. She leaned to her left side, and then dug into her right pant pocket for her cell phone. She scrolled through her list of contacts and stopped on the name Crystal. Nicole ran her right thumb over the raised keys on her phone while she dragged her left index finger across her bottom lip. Nicole went back and forth in her mind on whether to press the send button or not. She looked up and saw a man reading a magazine. She looked to her left and saw a woman walking slowly back and forth while talking on the phone. A car wash attendant walked briskly into the waiting room and said, "Blue Ford Focus." The man reading the magazine raised his right hand and said, "Right here." He and the attendant left the waiting room together.

Nicole returned her attention to her phone. The screen was black. She illuminated the screen with a click of one the phone's side buttons. Nicole closed her eyes and began to fantasize the same fantasy she'd been imagining since she was in middle school: the wedding that she and Crystal would have. She pictured Crystal's neatly pressed hair pulled into an up-do, and soft brown eyes and brown skin under a white veil. Nicole was snapped back to reality when she heard another car wash attendant call out, "Tan Chevy Camaro." The woman who was pacing while talking into her cell phone walked to the attendant and then they left together. Nicole went back to the list of contacts on her phone. Crystal's name came up. Nicole immediately pressed send. Nicole was doing what she hadn't done in four years, and that was to reach out to Crystal. The phone rang once then the sound of an ascending tone vibrated through her ear. "The number you have reached has been disconnected." Nicole's heart sunk.

"Peach Cadillac DeVille," an attendant called out. Silence. The attendant stepped up to Nicole who was the only person in the waiting room. "Are you the peach Cadillac DeVille?" the attendant asked. Nicole usually disliked when people referred to the cashmere color as peach. To her, cashmere sounded sophisticated, while peach sounded amateurish. She was too distracted to be annoyed. She stood up and walked out with the attendant in a state of shock.

Later that day, Nicole walked into Jasmine's Beauty Mart where Kurt Franklin's "Brighter Day" was playing from the store's speakers.

"Welcome to Jasmine's, sir ... err, miss," the clerk behind the register said to Nicole.

Nicole nodded and said, "Thank you," revealing her feminine voice. The clerk figured she had her gender right the second time.

Nicole saw the pictures that Ms. Anne had told her about but she decided to wander around the store a bit. She wanted to clear Crystal out of her head. Nicole saw the usual crochet knit skullcaps in the Pan-African colors of red, black, and green. She walked past the display of Hawaiian Silky relaxer. The scent of a mixture of incense caught her attention when she was about to reach the room containing a large collection of wigs. She stopped at the rack that held the incense. She twirled it around reading the name of woody-scented incenses. She halted the rack when she came to the fruity scents. Nicole began inhaling one package after another, trying to find one that appealed to her. From the corner of her right eye she saw someone a few feet from her walk to a display of shower caps. Nicole turned slightly to get a better look with one of the packages held to her nose. She saw black high heel boots that had black leggings tucked into them. Her eyes saw a long lavender sweater a few inches above the boots. The sweater wrapped around a voluptuous butt. A thick black belt was wrapped around a thin waist. Nicole's interest piqued. She saw French manicured nails framing a package of shower caps. Nicole's eyes made their way to the person's head where thick wavy black hair concealed the face of its owner. Nicole felt herself getting warm.

"Hey, man, who cut your hair?"

Nicole's attention was taken away by an unfamiliar male voice. She turned to see a teenage boy standing beside her, appreciating her haircut.

"My pops hooked me up," Nicole replied.

The teenager nodded, "That's what's up. A yo, does he have a shop somewhere?"

Nicole noticed the object of her earlier study looking up at the two of them talking. Nicole turned to see arched eyebrows, doe-shaped eyes framing black eyes, button nose, and full lips that shined from the black cherry lip-gloss that covered them. Nicole was taken. The woman, noticing Nicole's attention on her, smiled to reveal a set of straight white teeth that seemed to sparkle.

Nicole lowered the incense from her nose but did not remove her attention when she answered, "Nah man, nothing like that. He just trims me up every now and then."

"You lucky, man. You, lucky," the teenager said as he cupped one hand over the other and lifted his hands towards Nicole.

Nicole thanked him. The young man turned to walk down an aisle that was next to him.

"Are you just going to keep staring at me or are you going to say hello," the woman inquired.

Nicole swallowed.

"Hello," Nicole said.

The woman walked towards Nicole. The warmth that Nicole once felt was now feeling like heat.

"My name is Sheila. What's your name?"

"Uhm, Nicole."

The two women shook hands.

"You had to think about it. Is that your real name?"

"No. I mean, yeah. I mean." Nicole stopped talking. *Breath. Calm down,* Nicole thought. She straightened herself up and said more confidently, "My name is Nicole. What's yours?"

Sheila giggled, "I already told you, Sheila."

Nicole felt like an idiot.

"Do you live around here?" Sheila asked.

Okay, she's still talking to you. You can do this. "Yes. I live a few minutes from here. How about you?"

"I don't live too far from here either. I don't think I've ever seen you around."

"No. I'm pretty much either at work or studying."

"Oh, for real? What do you do and what are you studying?"

"I work for a bank doing stuff with checks. I study at the U of M. Business administration. How about you?"

"I am a hairstylist. I'm also in school, getting my nail technician license. I hope to someday own my own salon instead of renting a chair in someone else's. So you came in here to buy some incense?"

Nicole looked down at the package in her hand. "No. Actually, I came in here to get a picture for my place."

"You have your own place?"

"Yeah."

"You live alone or with roommates?"

"Alone."

Sheila took in Nicole. She liked what she saw and even more, she like what she was hearing.

"You want some help picking out a picture?"

Hell, yeah! "I would like that," Nicole said coolly.

The two women smiled at one another for a moment. They then made their way down the aisle towards the pictures.

CHAPTER THREE

The following evening, Nicole sat on her loveseat that was at the foot of her bed. She scrolled through her list of contacts and located Sheila's name. She pressed send.

"Hello."

"Hey, Sheila. It's me, Nicole. How are you?"

"I'm good now that you called. I was wondering how long it was going to take for you to ring my phone."

"I wasn't going to wait too long. I can't risk someone else stepping up in front of me."

Nicole wondered if she was assuming too much as the words left her mouth. She had no idea if Sheila was even "family" or not.

"No need to worry there."

"Why not?"

Sheila paused for a moment. She then released the words, "Not too many people are rushing to be in a relationship with a bisexual woman." Sheila closed her eyes and waited for Nicole's response.

All sorts of thoughts swam through Nicole's mind. She was excited to hear that she was in the "family". She was also pleased to hear that she was single. Lastly, Nicole was impressed that Sheila was honest about being bisexual. Most of the women Nicole had dated lied about their sexuality. This truthfulness was refreshing for Nicole.

"Silence. I understand. Not too many people are fond of people like me. You don't have to make any excuses. I'll just hang up and leave you alone," Sheila said dolefully.

"Wait! Don't hang up. I don't care you're bi. If anything, I am impressed you would even admit it. People usually say things like 'I don't believe in labels' when they don't want to admit their sexuality. I like that you own it."

Sheila perked up.

"Nice. What would you label yourself as?"

"Easy. Lesbian. I'm a soft stud. I like men's clothing. My style is masculine but I also like my female parts. Lastly, I treat woman the way men are expected to treat a lady. That is unless a woman teaches me she'd rather be treated differently."

"Interesting. So are you a touch-me-not?"

"Hell no. You can touch me anywhere you want."

"Anywhere?"

"Anywhere."

"Are you single?"

"Very single."

The two women breathed into their phones not believing their luck.

Nicole swung her legs onto her loveseat to get more comfortable. Nicole stared at the picture she and Sheila picked out the day before. The picture was of a black couple embracing in the orange glow of a sunset. Sheila, who was once sitting on her bed, lay on her stomach so she too was in a more comfortable position.

"What kind of things do you do for fun?" Nicole asked.

"I like to spend time with my family and friends. I always try to make it to my parents' each weekend for a meal."

"Me too. I love to cook for my family."

"You cook?"

"Yeah. How about you?"

Sheila closed her eyes then placed her free hand over them. "I can cook hotdogs," Sheila said with embarrassment. "But I do love to eat."

"If you bring your appetite, I will bring the food."

"It's a deal."

The two women fell into a comfortable conversation. They shared their likes, dislikes, and wants for their future. Nicole felt click after click after click when new similarities were discovered between the two of them. She was amazed with how comfortable Sheila was with herself. Her confidence was invigorating for Nicole.

Things were humming along until Sheila said, "I hope to one day be married, have a beautiful house, and a big pretty rock on my wedding ring."

Nicole sat up straight, "I'm not promising you anything. I barely know you. You barely know me," Nicole said with urgency.

Sheila was taken aback by Nicole's immediate words.

"I didn't say anything about wanting you to promise me anything."

"I'm just saying. Nothing in life is guaranteed. So I am not promising anything."

"Okaaay. It's been noted," Sheila said, trying to figure out what was going on.

There was an awkward silence.

Sheila broke the silence by saying, "Well, would you like to hang out sometime?" The question was both an invite and a way for Sheila to gauge if Nicole was still interested in her.

Nicole didn't respond right away. She was weighing the pros and cons. She eventually said, "Sure. I would like that. I have school and work all week. Does next Saturday work for you?"

A still puzzled Sheila said yes.

The two said their goodbyes and hung up. Nicole rubbed her head, staring at her ceiling. She hoped the future had good things in store for her. Her mind drifted to all the disappointments she had experienced in her life. The disappointments were from failed relationships with people inside and outside her family. Nicole was sick and tired of being disappointed. She wanted life to deal her a new deck of cards. *A few cards with my happy face on it would be nice,* she thought.

Nicole stood up from her loveseat and walked over to her kitchenette to pour herself a glass of ice water. She drank the beverage. The cold of the water energized her. Blood rushed to her head and provided momentum to get her mental wheels turning.

Nicole sat at her small dining table. She began to make plans for her date with Sheila. Plans she hoped would help reveal if Sheila was really down with her or expecting a free ride.

CHAPTER FOUR

The whole week seemed to have dragged by for Nicole. Everyday felt like Monday. Nicole thought Saturday would never show up. But once it did, it came with a vengeance. Minutes felt like seconds, hours felt like minutes. Before she knew it, she was sixty minutes, which felt to her as sixty seconds, away from seeing Sheila again. The date that she was looking forward to was now a source of anxiety for her. Nicole had clammy hands and a dry mouth. Her nerves vibrated throughout her body. The vibration made her feel as though it was shutting down. It was as if this was her final moments before she would either die or pass out. There was only one thing she knew to do in situations like this. She walked over to her stereo and put on Eminem's "Lose Yourself" to help her to be fearless to go after what she wanted: a fulfilling relationship. Nicole felt a vibration on her hip. At first she thought her nerves had decided to go into overdrive in that region of her body. She soon realized it was her phone receiving a text message. She read the message: *Good luck on your date tonight. Remember to relax and be yourself. We love you.*

Nicole smiled as she felt a cloud of calm come over her after she read the message from Ms. Anne.

Nicole wrote back: *Thx. I needed 2 hear that. I luv u guys 2.*

Nicole placed her phone back into the holder on her hip and turned off the music. Feeling pumped yet calm she walked out her front door and into the unknown.

The sky had a golden glow as the sun began to set. Nicole listened to the sounds of children playing in a front yard that was next to the duplex that she was parked in front of. She took note of how she managed to hold onto her pumped and calm feeling for the twenty minutes it took her to arrive at Sheila's place. She looked over at the passenger seat to make sure it was clean and clear of debris. She then sniffed the air to ensure the scent of strawberry could be detected from the car fragrance she tucked under her seat.

"Have fun, girl!" someone shouted from the bottom floor window of the duplex.

Nicole looked over and saw Sheila walking down the pathway to Nicole's car. She had on a grey crocheted beanie. Her black wavy hair rolled from under her hat down to her shoulders. A form-fitting pink knit long sleeved sweater covered her torso. A beige scarf partially covered the outline of her thirty-six double D breasts. The scarf fell to her waistline that was cloaked by a pair of form-fitting grey jeans. Her jeans were tucked into beige-colored high-heeled boots. Sheila could have easily been strutting herself down the path like Naomi Campbell on a runway because she looked that good. However, Sheila walked calmly to the car in an unassuming way. That melted Nicole's heart. Nicole jumped out of her car and walked over to the passenger side door. She opened it for the beauty, who she hoped would soon be her one-and-only.

"Awe, ain't that cute!" the same unknown person shouted from the window.

Sheila held back a laugh. Her dark brown skin hid the fact she was flushed with red from the embarrassment of the shouts coming from the window.

Nicole climbed back into the car. She quickly wished she hadn't put the strawberry fragrance under her seat because Sheila's floral perfume was stimulating.

"You look amazing, Sheila."

"Thanks. You don't look too shabby yourself. So where are you taking me?"

Nicole thought about the plans she had made. She was hesitant about revealing them to Sheila as she was beginning to have second thoughts.

"We'll see," Nicole said as she started the car.

"Don't do anything I wouldn't do!" the voice from the window shouted loud enough to ensure she was heard over the start of the car's engine.

Sheila could no longer hold her laughter. She cracked up.

"Who is doing all that hollering?" Nicole asked.

"That's my younger sister. She's just really excited for me."

"I guess we both have family members excited for us." Nicole pulled away from the curb and headed towards downtown Detroit.

Moments later, Nicole maneuvered her car through the quiet streets on the edge of downtown.

"I remember back in the day when this town used to be jumping with action."

"Yeah, me too."

"Bit of ghost town these days."

"It has its pockets."

Nicole rounded a corner where a Tubbies Fried Chicken stood. Sheila's body was expecting for the car to continue straight. She was shocked when her body moved to the right as Nicole made a left turn into the parking lot of Tubbies Fried Chicken. Sheila stopped breathing. Nicole parked in one of the many available parking spots and cut the engine. Horror swept through Sheila's body. The muffled sounds of the cashier repeating an order over the drive-thru intercom could be heard.

Sheila managed to say, "Nicole, what are we doing here?"

Nicole rubbed her forehead with her right hand.

"I just wanted to be sure. But after seeing you, our conversation, your energy, it just doesn't seem right anymore."

Sheila's body was stiff as if she was prepared for the boogey man to jump out at any moment. "You've lost me. What are you talking about?" Sheila asked. The prospect of having a first date dinner at a fast food chain horrified her. It was not her idea of romantic. She had pictured an intimate candlelit dinner where they could get to know one another more. A family-friendly bright restaurant was not what she had in mind.

Nicole began tapping her fingers along the slope of her forehead with her eyes closed.

"I wanted to be sure you want to be with me for me. Not for what you think I can provide you with. I don't want to set high expectations for the future."

"Nicole, the only thing I was expecting was to go out with you tonight and have a good time. Not to say we couldn't have a good time at," Sheila turned to look at a family with eager kids running towards the restaurant, "Tubbies, but come on. You have to give me a chance."

"Ugh. You here it all the time, right?"

"You hear what all the time." Sheila was beginning to think that Nicole was hearing voices.

"Let bygones be bygones. Don't live in the past, live for the future."

Sheila no longer thought she was in a car with a crazy person. She understood where Nicole was going with the conversation and what she was feeling.

"Don't let people from your past interfere with your future." Sheila looked down at her pants. "It's hard to do sometimes," she said as she fidgeted with the seam of her scarf.

Without thinking, Nicole took Sheila's left hand into her right hand and squeezed it softly.

"Yes. It is."

They both looked at each other in a way that said they both understood each other.

"Let's get out of here," Nicole said as she started the car and began to back up.

"Are you sure? I mean, there's probably a drumstick sitting in there with your name on it."

"No. Let's go somewhere else."

Sheila breathed a sigh of relief.

CHAPTER FIVE

Nicole and Sheila were walking down a sparsely-populated street the following Saturday morning. The warmth from the coffee swishing around in Nicole's travel mug warmed her right hand.

"You know, you really didn't need to do this. I enjoyed our date after we left Tubbies last week. The view from that hotel's restaurant was breathtaking, the food was delicious, and the company was excellent," Sheila said.

"I agree. I just want us to have a date that is perfect from the beginning to the end."

"Why does it have to end?"

Nicole wanted to say that all good things must come to an end. Instead she said, "It doesn't have to."

The women walked a block more when Sheila stopped at a door of a building that had large windows. Nicole peered into the window and saw an assortment of beads.

"Okay. So where are we?"

"It's a bead store."

"What are we doing at a bead store?"

"Well, you said I could choose whatever I wanted us to do, right?"

"Yeah," Nicole said apprehensively.

"Well, this is what I want to do."

"Buy some beads."

"Yes, and I signed us up for a jewelry-making class."

"A what making class?"

The shock of what Nicole was hearing woke her up quicker than the caffeinated beverage she had been sipping.

"A jewelry-making class. Now come on, it will be fun."

"But I don't wear jewelry. Just my watch."

"Then you can make me something."

The thought of making Sheila something changed something in Nicole. She liked the idea of making a piece of jewelry Sheila could adorn herself with.

Nicole opened and held the door for Sheila. Nicole felt cautious excitement when she followed Sheila into the store.

Sheila was in her element. The vast assortment of beads had her creative mind going a hundred miles an hour. The possibilities were endless. Nicole on the other hand was overwhelmed. There were so many different colors, textures, and shininess.

"I'm going to make it easy for you," Sheila said to a shell-shocked Nicole.

Sheila reached up towards a display of kits to get something that caught her eye. She pulled down a garland bracelet kit. The kit contained orange, brown, and peach beads. She then retrieved a beginner's bracelet kit for Nicole.

Nicole followed Sheila to the register to pay for their items. The cashier rang them up. She then asked, "Are you two taking the bracelet-making class?"

Sheila replied with a yes.

"Then that means you get ten-percent off of your purchase today. Will you need any of the tools?"

"No. We have our own," Sheila responded as she patted the side of her purse.

The cashier gave them their total. Before Sheila could take out her wallet Nicole whipped her billfold out and paid for the items.

"I have lunch," Sheila said.

Nicole smiled and said, "Okay."

Nicole and Sheila entered the classroom where mostly middle-aged woman were sitting waiting for the instructor to begin. Nicole watched as Sheila expertly rolled out her mat and tools in front of her. She did the same for an extra set she brought for Nicole. Sheila introduced Nicole to all of the tools, even though her beginner's kit didn't require the use of most of them.

"How do you know all this stuff?" Nicole inquired.

"My sister and I make jewelry together when we have time. We've been doing it since we were kids."

"So is all the jewelry you wear your own creations?"

"Most of them are."

Sheila then opened the kit for Nicole and spread the contents out before her. Nicole's eyes lit up when she saw her school's colors, blue and yellow. Sheila then spread her own kit's contents before her. Nicole noted the sparkle in her beads and the lack thereof in her own.

"Why are your beads so sparkly?"

"Mine are Swarovski crystals. Your beads are plastic."

"I don't want plastic I want the cool looking ones like yours."

"You must work your way up to get to this level."

Nicole leaned over to Sheila. "I'll work my way up alright," Nicole said with a whisper into Sheila's ear.

Sheila felt herself getting excited.

"Shh, I think the instructor is about to start."

At the end of the class, Sheila had created a garland bracelet she was proud of. She had just the outfit in mind she would where with it. Nicole was happy with her creation merely because it contained her school's colors. She was finished with her simple bracelet before the rest of the class. She ended up helping Sheila hold certain strands and beads in place as she tied there and snipped there. That was Nicole's favorite part of the class, the two of them creating something together.

Sheila eyed Nicole's bracelet. "I like your masterpiece. When do I get to wear it?"

"You can wear it now," Nicole replied as she opened the clasp and moved the piece of jewelry towards Sheila. She proceeded to secure the clasp onto Sheila's wrist.

Sheila moved her wrist side to side, admiring the bracelet. "I like it. You did a good job. So the class didn't kill you now, did it?"

"Thanks, and no, it didn't. I actually had a good time."

"Me too. So where to next?"

"It's time for lunch, and I have a spot in mind."

"Wait, don't tell me. I know, another amazing fast-food place," Sheila said sarcastically.

"No. I have something else in store. Have you ever had food from the gas station? They have the bomb food there," Nicole said jokingly.

"I swear, Nicole, if you take me to a gas station I am going to scream," Sheila said as she gave Nicole's shoulder a playful soft slap.

Nicole nudged Sheila with her shoulder to hers, "Hey don't knock gas station food. It can be on the gourmet side." Nicole couldn't keep the straight face she wanted to have. She ended up cracking up.

"Yeah, right," Sheila said as she joined in Nicole's laughter.

CHAPTER SIX

Three months later, Sheila woke up in Nicole's bed. She reached over to the nightstand for a tin box that held breath mints. She slipped one into her mouth. Sheila felt Nicole stir. She then felt the warmth of her body as she began to spoon her. Sheila placed her right hand on top of Nicole's right hand.

"Good morning to the graduate. How does it feel to be officially educated?" she asked.

Nicole slid her right hand under Sheila nightshirt. Her hand made its way to Sheila's right breast. Nicole found comfort in its warmth and softness. She began to massage it.

"It feels good."

Sheila closed her eyes as her nipples began to get perky.

"Hey, we don't have time for this," Sheila said softly.

"Yes, we do," Nicole gently protested.

"No, we don't," Sheila replied. She lifted herself up from the bed and threw back the cover from her body.

Nicole retreated when the cool air joined her under the warm comforter.

"We have to get ready to go. I don't want to be late for your graduation party. I also want to help out with setting up. I don't want your mom and dad thinking I'm a lazy good for nothing."

"My family likes you."

"How do you know?"

Nicole reached over to her nightstand and retrieved her phone. She handed it to Sheila. "Look at the last text."

Sheila began to say something when Nicole said, "Just flip it open and look at my last message."

Sheila did as instructed. She saw a message from Ms. Anne and read: *Sheila is a keeper* ☺

Sheila smiled and handed the phone back to Nicole who also had a grin on her face.

"Well, they just met me at the graduation ceremony last night. We didn't really get a chance to talk with each other. Today, I want to

really make a good impression. Second impressions are everything,"
Sheila said as she hurried to the bathroom.

"Okay, okay whatever you say."

Nicole dragged herself out of bed to start her day.

Nicole's peach cobbler was looking like a million bucks to
Charles. He was hoping his daughter would bring her homemade
dessert to the backyard graduation party being held at his home.

Ms. Anne attempted several times to make her cobbler as
delicious as Nicole's but could never achieve the same degree of
satisfying taste. She would use more or less butter here and there add
a sprinkle of cinnamon, used canned peaches in heavy syrup, and
then used fresh peaches in her own sugary sauce. Charles would raise
his eyebrows and make the sounds of hmm then say okay, as he
tasted his wife's creations. He would then take a napkin and wipe an
invisible something from his mouth. Being the loving trooper he was,
he would then make a second attempt at his wife's efforts. Ms. Anne
could see her husband's troubles and could clearly see he wasn't
looking at the dessert like it was a million bucks but rather a tarnished
penny lying alone on one of Detroit's dirty sidewalks. Ms. Anne
would then thank Charles for being nice then proceed to remove the
cobbler, or tarnished penny, from his presence. Today, Ms. Anne
decided she was going to ask Nicole for the recipe.

Nicole, Sheila, and Malcolm were conversing when Ms. Anne
walked up to Nicole and asked if she could have a moment with her.
Nicole left but soon returned after she wrote down the recipe for her
peach cobbler for Ms. Anne.

Upon her return, Nicole heard Malcolm say, "So did you have
fun celebrating your three-month anniversary?" Malcolm asked
Sheila.

Sheila had a puzzled look on her face when she said, "I didn't
know people celebrated three-month anniversaries."

Nicole interrupted the conversation by saying, "Malcolm, it was
supposed to be a surprise."

"We are celebrating three months?" Sheila asked.

"Yeah, I wanted to surprise you tonight."

Sheila resisted the urge to give Nicole a peck on the cheek to
show her appreciation. She was still concerned about making her
good second impression that she settled with saying thank you.

Malcolm was tickled by what he saw between his sister and Sheila. He noted that he hadn't seen her happy like this before. Even with Crystal, she wasn't so relaxed and natural. Without warning, the tender moment was pierced by a commotion coming from the entryway into the backyard.

Nicole turned her attention to a group of people entering the party. There were shouts of "Where's the graduate?" from a couple of them. They looked to be drunk.

"Looks like the party's about to get started," a somewhat familiar female voice said.

Nicole narrowed her eyes while she attempted to figure out who was making all the noise. "Yeah, it looks as if it is," a male voice responded.

Like a heat-seeking missile, Nicole's eyes locked onto a familiar face. It was a face she had not seen in nine years. Her mouth dropped open.

Malcolm saw the same person. He placed his left hand on Nicole's right shoulder.

"Martha," Nicole said faintly. Nicole didn't know if she should run and hide, or walk up to the woman and give her biological mother a sharp slap across her face.

Nicole's father appeared out of nowhere and blocked Nicole's view of Martha.

Nicole's mind drifted back to the arguments Marshal and Martha had over Nicole's tomboyish style and ways. The repeated put-downs that Martha would say to her daughter. Nicole's body began to quiver from the remembrance of her mother's rejection of her. Nicole feared that the hateful remarks that Martha spewed privately in their home would now be displayed for all to see. Nicole felt ashamed. She felt exposed.

The partygoers that included Nicole's close friends and family were now a captive audience.

Nicole snapped back to the present moment when she heard her father say, "Why are you here?"

"I'm family, ain't I?" Martha replied as she took a drag from the cigarette that dangled between her index and middle finger.

Nicole started a slow walk towards her father whose back was still blocking a full view of Martha. A concerned, Sheila reached out to stop Nicole but Malcolm held her hand back. Nicole reached the side of Marshal. From there, she was able to see how Martha had not aged gracefully. She looked rougher and meaner than ever before. She had the same relaxed hair but there were streaks of grey that had replaced her once brilliant black hair. The parts of Martha's eyes that used to contain white now held deep brown-yellowish and red streaks.

"Who told you where we live?" Marshal looked at the family members that arrived with Martha. His cousin, Herald said, "You know how persistent Martha can be, man."

Marshal shook his head at his cousin.

"What? Why you actin' like you don't want me here?" Martha said begrudgingly.

"Because I don't. In fact, none of us want you here."

The wind changed and Nicole began to smell the putrid stench of alcohol, cigarettes, and filth coming off of Martha. Nicole wrinkled her nose.

Martha looked Nicole up and down. "I see she's still dressin' like a nigga," Martha slurred.

Marshal clinched his fist.

Martha turned her attention to Marshal and Ms. Anne's home. "Well aint' that about a bitch. You got yourself this fancy new house. I saw your fancy car out front. So you must think you too good for a bitch, huh?" Martha continued.

Ms. Anne walked out to the backyard from the kitchen. She was startled to see Martha. Ms. Anne threw a concerned look at Marshal when she saw Martha. Marshal gave her a look that said he had it under control. Martha looked at Ms. Anne's wedding ring.

Martha felt tears rolling around the bottom and corners of her eyes. "Ya'll motherfuckas ain't shit," she shouted. Streaks of pain struck each word.

A remorseful Harold went up to Martha. He attempted to usher her out without causing her to resist. "Hey Martha, maybe we ought to go hit up one of the casinos in Windsor," Harold suggested.

Martha took a drag from her cigarette. She then flicked it towards Marshal where it bounced off his chest then fell to the ground. Martha then looked Nicole square in her eyes. "Yeah ain't shit goin' on here," she said.

Martha's insult pierced Nicole's heart but she said nothing in her own defense. Something in her told her it wasn't worth it.

Martha began to walk out of the backyard with Harold behind her. Harold turned to face Marshal and mouthed the words, "Sorry, man."

"Oh, hold up. Hold up. Wait one minute. How I could I forget my present to the birthday boy," Martha said as she spun around on her heels and staggered back to the place she once stood a few seconds ago. No one felt the need to correct Martha's mention of birthday.

"Now I just happened to see no other than that girl, what her name?" Martha thought hard for a moment. "Crystal," she answered her own question.

Nicole's attention heightened. Sheila's heart dropped as she anticipated Crystal, Nicole's first love, to come running into the drama that was unfolding in the backyard like some kind of champ.

"I saw that girl's mother. And boy did she look like a hot mess. Crack done took its toll on that woman," Martha said apparently unaware of her own appearance. "You wouldn't believe what she told me about Crystal," Martha continued. "Well, I'll just let ya'll read about it since I can see my presence isn't wanted here."

Martha proceeded to reach into her back pocket. She took a piece of paper out and threw it to the ground.

"Happy merry birthday, boy," Martha said wickedly to Nicole as she turned on her heels and exited. Harold and the other unwelcomed guests were close behind.

Marshall ran and snatched the paper up before Nicole had a chance to take one step towards it. Marshal unfolded the paper. He saw that it was an online news article.

The headline read: *Fatal Three-car Accident on I-480 East*. Marshal then read the words: Omaha, Nebraska. His heart thumped rapidly when he saw a picture of Crystal with the caption, "Deceased mother of two-year old," beneath it. Marshal said damn under his breath.

Nicole saw the sorrowful look on her father's face. She snatched the paper from his hand and read the article. Nicole was in disbelief when her legs weakened. She fell to her knees and sobbed.

CHAPTER SEVEN

The following week was a blur for Nicole. She frantically attempted to find out the details of what happened to Crystal. All the while, she was ignoring calls from her parents. She also ignored a call from Sheila. Nicole did not allow anything or anyone to get in her way of trying to find out what happened to her first love. She had questions that she needed answered. Why was Crystal in Nebraska? Crystal told her she was moving to Missouri. Where was Jerome? The article gave no mention of him. And where was Crystal's daughter?

Nicole's search began in the neighborhood where she and Crystal grew up. She went to Crystal's old apartment building hoping she would be able to get in contact with her mom. It had only been about four years since she was last there but things had changed a lot. The neighborhood had become dirtier. There were weeds coming up between the cracks in the sidewalks and potholes in the streets that looked like ancient dried-up lakebeds.

Nicole saw a man exiting Crystal's former apartment building. She gave him Crystal's mom's information in hopes he knew where to find her. He didn't. Nicole continued to wander around the street asking person after person if they knew anything. No one did.

She then began inquiring about Jerome. People were very familiar with him but had no desire to reveal any information about a drug dealer who still had ties in the neighborhood.

All of Nicole's efforts were fruitless.

In despair, Nicole headed back to her home to see what she could dig up on the Internet. She searched for the number to the Nebraska state highway patrol. The only response that anyone would give her was that all public information was released to the public via the media outlets. No further information could be provided. Nicole slammed the phone down in frustration.

She then began dialing hospital after hospital. She inquired about Crystal and her child. Each hospital gave the same privacy reasons for not disclosing any information regarding a patient whether or not they were actually at that hospital or another. The only way they would say anything is if Nicole could prove she was kin. Nicole was not, and she soon found herself in yet another dead end.

Nicole noted to herself towards the end of the week that it was as if that chapter in her life was over. There was no going back. There was also no going down the path she once thought was possible with Crystal. It was as if she was being nudged to move on. Nicole had no choices left. The only thing she could do was to grieve the loss of Crystal.

CHAPTER EIGHT

Two weeks later, the afternoon sun's heat bounced off the parking lot's pavement and unto Sheila's perspiring face. She was unable to park close to Nicole's front door. Instead, she found herself walking about a block to her building with a grocery bag in tow. Sheila looked around the street amazed there were so many cars parked. It was evidence that people were choosing to stay indoors rather than risk melting in the heat. Sheila hoped Nicole would answer her door. She attempted to see Nicole a few days after the Martha incident but Nicole wanted to be left alone. Ms. Anne and Marshal reached out to Sheila and assured her Nicole would be okay, and she just needed some space to absorb all that had happened. Sheila respected her girlfriend's wishes and stayed away. This was Sheila's first attempt in two weeks to reach out to Nicole.

Sheila made it to the air-conditioned entryway of Nicole's building. She dropped the grocery bag down on the ground, held her arms out, and tilted her head back to allow the cool air to circulate around her heated, moist body. A man walked out of the security door and held it open for Sheila. She thanked him and walked in with grocery bag in hand. She then thought it better to at least allow Nicole the decision of whether or not she wanted her knocking on her door. Sheila opened the security door and propped it open with the bag. She then dialed Nicole's door code. To her surprise, Nicole answered.

"Hello."

"Hey Nicole, it's me Sheila. I just wanted to stop by to say hey."

Nicole did not respond.

Sheila heard the sound of the door buzzing, indicating that Nicole had let her in.

Sheila said yes to herself. She went to the elevator bank and pressed the up button. She thought about what she would say to Nicole when she saw her. She wondered if her apartment was in disarray. Her mind then began to think that maybe Nicole would dump her, citing she wasn't ready for a relationship after what had happened. Sheila began to doubt what she was doing was the appropriate thing to do. She thought about turning around to head back to her car. She looked through the windows of the security doors. The blazing heat was not a place she wanted to walk back into again. The elevator door beeped a few times, indicating its arrival. Sheila stepped in.

Sheila watched the elevator numbers ascend to five. She stepped off the elevator and headed to Nicole's door. Sheila held her head down low, wondering what she was about to walk into. She began to see a figure standing in the hall as she walked closer to Nicole's door. She lifted her head to see Nicole. Sheila wasn't close enough to see what type of expression she had on her face. The closer she got the more she could see that it contained a faint smile. Nicole began to walk a few steps towards Sheila. She embraced her once she was close enough to do so. Sheila was relieved.

"I missed you, baby," Sheila said.

"I missed you too," Nicole replied.

Nicole took the bag from Sheila. "What do you have in here?" Nicole asked.

"Just a few things. I came over to cook for you."

Nicole raised her eyebrows in disbelief. "For real? What are you about to cook?"

"My specialty."

Soon Nicole's apartment was filled with the smell of boiling hotdogs. Sheila moved clumsily around the kitchen as she retrieved a pitcher and large spoon. She poured in water, two packs of fruit punch flavored Kool-Aid, and a few cups of sugar. She stirred until everything was dissolved. Sheila turned her attention to the boiling hotdogs. She turned the burner off, and placed the hotdogs onto buns that were resting on plates. Sheila then tossed tortilla chips onto the plates, and set them on a small table that was between the bed and kitchenette.

Nicole watched her girlfriend from the table serve her. She was humored by her efforts. Sheila then dropped ice cubes in glasses and poured the Kool-Aid in. She carefully walked back to the table with the beverages in hand.

Sheila sat down and sighed. "Well, how do they say it? Bon appétit."

"Yeah, baby, bon appétit," Nicole said as she took Sheila's hand in hers. "Red Kool-Aid, chips, and hotdogs. I didn't know I was going to be so lucky today," Nicole said as she reached for the condiments that were sitting in the middle of the table.

"I know it's not much."

"Hey, it's a lot coming from you. Thank you, I really appreciate this. So how have you been?"

"I've been okay. Thinking about you a lot. Hoping you were okay," Sheila said as she bit into a chip.

"I'm okay now. I just had to make sense of everything that happened."

Sheila was curious about what conclusions she was able to come to.

Nicole squirted ketchup onto her hotdog. "I felt ashamed knowing that you saw the ills of my family. My stuff was just aired out there. But in the end, I came to realize there was nothing for me to be ashamed of. You know, that's my birth mom. There's nothing I can do to change the past or change how she is presently. Seeing how she turned out just made me that more grateful for the good I have in my life. I like the person I've become. Who's to say I wouldn't have the good life I have if it wasn't for those experiences." Nicole took a bite out of her hotdog.

"You came to all of this in just two weeks?"

"No, I am sure it has been forming for a while. I think the incident just made things clearer for me."

Sheila played with a chip, "And what about Crystal."

"It saddens me that such a kind person is no longer with us. I tried to find out what happened to her child but I couldn't get anywhere with that because I'm not kin. I tried contacting her mom but she's nowhere to be found. I just pray her little girl is okay. That's all I can do is pray and move on because it is beyond my control."

Sheila saw that Nicole was okay. She felt her spirits lighten up. Sheila continued eating her meal.

Nicole felt something profound stirring inside of her as she watched Sheila eat. Nicole looked at the pot that contained the boiling hotdogs. She then turned her attention back to Sheila. Nicole noted that sweat had turned Sheila's once wavy hair into stringy strands. Nicole pulled her chair over to Sheila. Sheila stopped eating. She had a confused look on her face as she turned her body to face Nicole.

"Hey you, I never stopped thinking about you. My parents told me you kept in contact with them to see how I was doing." Nicole grasped Sheila's hands, and lifted them up to kiss each of them.

"I just wanted to make sure you were okay," Sheila said with damp eyes.

Nicole stood up. Sheila stood up with her. Nicole wiped tears from Sheila's cheeks with her thumbs. She then began to kiss her girlfriend tenderly. Nicole soon began to feel a soothing rumble awaken something in her heart while Sheila began to feel a tender release within her soul. They both felt the sweetness of love growing deep within them.

About the Author

Ninamaste MaTuri is a Minnesotan who enjoys writing, and hopes to continue writing stories. She also enjoys hiking, visiting museums, and traveling in her spare time. She is author also of *The Preludes* and *Clear Sense*.

You can visit Ninamaste MaTuri at:
www.NinamasteMaTuri.com